Original Title: Asphalt and Glory

© Asphalt and Glory, Carlos Martínez Cerdá and Víctor Martínez Cerdá, 2023

Authors: Víctor Martínez Cerdá and Carlos Martínez Cerdá (V&C Brothers)

© Cover and illustrations: V&C Brothers

Layout and design: V&C Brothers

ASPHALT AND GLORY

THE MOST ICONIC
FORMULA 1 DRIVERS

Table of Contents

25. Jochen Rindt.

26. Gilles Villeneuve.

27. Stirling Moss.

28. Emerson Fittipaldi.

29. Carlos Sainz.

30. Esteban Ocon.

31. Jackie Ickx.

32. Jody Scheckter.

33. Jacques Villeneuve.

34. Heikki Kovalainen.

35. Felipe Massa.

36. Pastor Maldonado.

37. Robert Kubica.

38. David Coulthard.

39. Nico Hülkenberg.

40. Eddie Irvine.

41. Gerhard Berger.

42. Rubens Barrichello.

43. Jarno Trulli.

44. Lance Stroll.

45. Mick Schumacher.

46. Lando Norris.

47. George Russell.

MICHAEL SCHUMACHER

1

MICHAEL SCHUMACHER.

He is regarded as one of the most successful and iconic drivers in the history of Formula 1.

-Formula 1 Career: He competed in Formula 1 from 1991 to 2012, making him the longest-serving driver in the category. During this time, he drove for the Jordan, Benetton, and Ferrari teams, and also briefly returned with Mercedes.

-World Championships: He won a total of seven Formula 1 world championships, setting a record that stood as of my last update in September 2021. He clinched his titles with Benetton in 1994 and 1995, and then with Ferrari in 2000, 2001, 2002, 2003, and 2004.

-Records and Achievements: He holds multiple Formula 1 records, including the most Grand Prix wins (91), the most podium finishes (155), and the most fastest laps (77). He also held the record for pole positions until it was surpassed by Lewis Hamilton in 2020. Moreover, he topped the points table in six different seasons.

-Driving Style and Skills: He was known for his aggressiveness on the track and his ability to extract the maximum performance from his car. He was a cunning and strategic driver, able to quickly adapt to various conditions and seize opportunities during races.

-Health Status: Sadly, in December 2013, Schumacher suffered a severe skiing accident in the French Alps, resulting in a traumatic brain injury. Since then, his health condition has been kept private, with no up-to-date public information provided about his recovery.

Superstitions:

-Helmet: He always wore the same helmet for every race. It was red with a white and green stripe on top, representing the German flag. He considered his helmet a sort of lucky charm and refused to change its design over the years.

-**Number 7:** He had a fondness for the number 7. He used this number at various points in his career, both in his early years at Benetton and upon his return to Mercedes. Even after he retired, his son Mick Schumacher also chose the number 7 for his Formula 1 career.

-**Red socks:** He used to wear red socks during races. This was a personal ritual that gave him confidence and became a part of his racing attire.

-**Watch:** Before getting into the car, Schumacher used to take off his watch and give it to his wife or a member of his team. He did this as a way to fully concentrate on the race and avoid any distractions.

-**Left hand on the car:** He had the habit of touching the left side of his car as he got into it before every race. This was a kind of ritual to ensure he had a connection with his vehicle and to convey good luck.

Accidents:

-**Skiing accident (2013):** He had an accident while skiing at the Méribel ski resort in the French Alps. He hit his head against a rock and suffered a traumatic brain injury. He was urgently transported to the hospital and underwent several surgical procedures. Since then, he has been kept private, and little information about his health has been publicly disclosed.

-**Accident at Silverstone (1999):** During the British Grand Prix in 1999, Schumacher had an accident on the first lap of the race due to a collision with his teammate, Eddie Irvine. His car crashed violently into the tire barriers, and he suffered a fracture in his right leg. This forced him to miss much of the 1999 season.

-**Collision at the British Grand Prix (1994):** In the 1994 season, at the British Grand Prix, Schumacher collided with his rival Damon Hill during a battle for position on lap 46. Both cars were damaged and had to retire from the race. This incident was controversial, as Schumacher was disqualified for not allowing Hill to pass.

-Accident at the Australian Grand Prix (1995): In the first race
of the 1995 season in Australia, Schumacher crashed into
the wall after losing control of his car due to heavy rain.
The accident was dramatic, but Schumacher emerged unscathed.

Rivalries:

-Damon Hill: One of Schumacher's most renowned rivalries was
with Damon Hill, who was his main contender for the world
championship in the 1994 season. In the last race of that season,
the Australian Grand Prix, Schumacher and Hill were involved
in a race incident that ended with both drivers out of the
competition. Schumacher was disqualified from the
championship due to his involvement in the incident,
while Hill became the champion.

-Jacques Villeneuve: In the 1997 season, both drivers vied for
the world championship. At the European Grand Prix that year,
Schumacher attempted to block Villeneuve in an overtaking
maneuver but ended up colliding with the Canadian driver's car.
This incident resulted in Schumacher's disqualification from the
season, and Villeneuve clinched the title.

-Mika Hakkinen: Schumacher also had a fierce rivalry with Mika
Hakkinen, who was his main on-track rival during the late 1990s
and early 2000s. Both drivers engaged in several battles for the
championship and showcased thrilling duels on the track.
Although they had some tense moments, they also displayed
mutual respect and admiration.

LEWIS
HAMILTON

2

LEWIS HAMILTON.

Born on January 7, 1985, in Stevenage, Hertfordshire, United Kingdom, he is one of the most successful and recognized drivers in Formula 1 history.

-Formula 1 Debut: He made his Formula 1 debut in 2007 with the McLaren team. In his rookie season, he stunned everyone by fighting for the championship until the last race and finished second behind Kimi Räikkönen.

-World Championships: Hamilton has clinched multiple world championships in his career. Up to my knowledge cutoff in September 2021, he had won seven Formula 1 world championships, tying the record set by Michael Schumacher. He secured his championships in 2008, 2014, 2015, 2017, 2018, 2019, and 2020.

-Records and Achievements: Hamilton has set numerous records throughout his Formula 1 career.

Some of his notable accomplishments include:

-Most Grand Prix wins: Hamilton surpassed Michael Schumacher's record to become the driver with the most victories in Formula 1 history.

-Most pole positions: Hamilton has achieved a remarkable number of pole positions throughout his career, setting the record for the most pole positions in Formula 1 history.

-Most podiums in Formula 1: Hamilton also set a record by achieving the most podiums in Formula 1 history.

-Dominance with Mercedes Team: Since 2013, Hamilton has been racing for the Mercedes team, where he has displayed impressive dominance in Formula 1. He has won multiple championships and has been a key figure in the team's success.

-Activism and Voice on Social Issues: Hamilton is known for using his platform in Formula 1 to advocate for racial equality, social justice, and environmental sustainability. He has been vocal about issues such as diversity in sports and climate change.

-Driving Style and Skills: He is recognized for his natural talent and aggressive driving style. He excels in wet conditions and is considered a very well-rounded driver in terms of technical skills and on-track strategy.

Superstitions:

-Number 44: He has used the number 44 on his car for much of his Formula 1 career. He believes this number is his lucky number and has been consistent in his choice over the years.

-Crossing Fingers: Before each race, Hamilton has mentioned that he crosses the fingers of his right hand while sitting in the car. He does this as a ritual to attract good luck and remain focused on the race.

-Wearing Specific Clothing: Hamilton has a habit of wearing certain specific garments during race weekends. These items may include particular underwear or socks which he believes provide him with positive energy and confidence.

-Pet: He has a dog named Roscoe who often accompanies him at the races. Before getting into the car, Hamilton has mentioned that he pats his dog to relax and find peace before competing.

-Visualization and Meditation: Hamilton practices visualization and meditation techniques before races. This involves closing his eyes and picturing the track, his optimal performance, and success in the race. Meditation also helps to calm his mind and focus on the present.

Accidents:

-**Brazil Grand Prix 2007:** In his debut season in Formula 1, Hamilton was involved in an accident at the Brazil Grand Prix. Under heavy rain conditions, he went off the track and hit a tire barrier. However, he was able to continue in the race and secure the runner-up spot for the world championship.

-**Spain Grand Prix 2016:** During the first lap of the Spain Grand Prix in 2016, Hamilton and his teammate, Nico Rosberg, collided at turn 4 after a tussle for position. Both cars sustained significant damage and had to retire from the race. This incident led to additional tension in the relationship between Hamilton and Rosberg at the time.

-**Qualifying for the Belgium Grand Prix 2017:** During the qualifying session for the Belgium Grand Prix in 2017, Hamilton lost control of his car at turn 13 and crashed into the tire barriers. Although the crash was dramatic, Hamilton emerged unharmed and was able to participate in the race the following day.

-**Italy Grand Prix 2018:** On the first lap of the Italy Grand Prix in 2018, Hamilton collided with Sebastian Vettel's car as they vied for position at turn 4. The contact caused Vettel to spin and he had to rejoin the track from the last position. Hamilton was able to continue in the race and finished in second place.

Rivalries:

-**Nico Rosberg:** Hamilton's most notable rivalry was with his former Mercedes teammate, Nico Rosberg. Both drivers had a tense relationship while competing together in the Mercedes team from 2013 to 2016. Their rivalry reached its peak in the 2016 season, with several on-track incidents and internal team tensions. However, after Rosberg retired from Formula 1 at the end of that season, the relationship between the two improved.

-Sebastian Vettel: Hamilton has also had a rivalry with Sebastian Vettel, who primarily raced for the Ferrari team during much of Hamilton's tenure at Mercedes. Both drivers have clashed numerous times on the track, vying for championships and victories. While they've had some skirmishes and collisions, their rivalry has largely been respectful.

-Fernando Alonso: In the early years of Hamilton's career, he had a rivalry with Fernando Alonso, who was his teammate at McLaren in 2007. The relationship between them became strained due to internal team disputes and battles for supremacy. However, over the years, their rivalry has mellowed, and both drivers have shown mutual respect.

AYRTON SENNA DA SILVA

3

AYRTON SENNA DA SILVA.

Known as Ayrton Senna, he was a prominent Brazilian racing driver.

He was born on March 21, 1960, in São Paulo, Brazil, and tragically passed away on May 1, 1994, during the San Marino Grand Prix, at the Imola circuit, Italy.

He is regarded as one of the most talented and successful drivers in Formula 1 history.

He raced in Formula 1 for 10 seasons, from 1984 to 1994, representing the teams Toleman, Lotus, McLaren, and Williams.

Throughout his career, he secured a total of 41 Grand Prix wins and clinched three Formula 1 world championships in 1988, 1990, and 1991.

He was known for his aggressive and daring driving style, as well as his ability to deliver exceptional performances under challenging weather conditions.

Ayrton Senna gained recognition for his skill in extracting the utmost performance from the cars he raced and for his intensely competitive approach.

He was renowned for his dedication and passion for racing, and his constant pursuit of perfection led him to be considered one of the best drivers of his generation.

In addition to his success on the track, Senna was also recognized for his commitment to social and humanitarian causes.

He founded the Ayrton Senna Institute, a charitable organization aimed at helping to improve the education of children and youth in Brazil.

Superstitions:

-Yellow helmet: Senna always wore a distinctive yellow helmet during his races. The yellow color became his personal trademark, and he chose it because he believed it was more visible on the track, increasing his safety.

-Amulets and religious symbols: He was a deeply religious man and carried various amulets and religious symbols with him before races. These included a pendant of Our Lady of Aparecida, the patron saint of Brazil, and a wristband in Brazilian colors blessed by his sister.

-Race morning routine: He had a specific routine before each race. This included praying, reading the Bible, listening to classical music, and meditating to find the necessary calm and focus.

-Leaving the garage last: On some occasions, Senna insisted on being the last driver to leave the garage before the race. He believed this provided him with a mental edge by having a clear view of the track and avoiding distractions.

-Stone in the shoe: Before getting into the car, Senna would often place a small stone in his shoe as a symbolic act to "feel" the car and connect with the track.

Accidents:

-Monaco Grand Prix 1984: During the qualifying practice, Senna crashed his Toleman-Hart at the Portier corner, sidelining him from the session. However, this performance allowed him to stand out for his skill in the rain and earned him recognition in Formula 1.

-German Grand Prix 1984: Senna had an incident in the first lap of the race where he collided with Alain Prost's car, ending his participation in the race.

-Italian Grand Prix 1985: During the race in Monza, Senna had an accident at the Ascari chicane. Despite the impact, he emerged unscathed.

-Japan Grand Prix 1987: Senna crashed his Lotus-Honda during the warm-up lap due to a gearbox issue, sidelining him from the race.

-Japan Grand Prix 1989: In one of the most remembered battles in Formula 1 history, Senna and Prost collided at the first corner of the Suzuka circuit. The crash ended the race for both drivers and resulted in Prost securing the world championship.

-Ayrton Senna suffered a tragic accident during the San Marino Grand Prix on May 1, 1994, at the Imola circuit, Italy.
The accident took place at the Tamburello corner, one of the fastest sections of the track. On lap 7 of the race, Senna's car, a Williams-Renault, left the track at high speed and violently hit the retaining wall. The impact was extremely severe, and it was later discovered that one of the front suspension rods had pierced Senna's helmet, causing severe head injuries. Ayrton Senna was extracted from the car and quickly transported to the hospital, where resuscitation attempts were made, but tragically, they could not save his life. He was pronounced dead a few hours later due to the injuries sustained in the crash.
Senna's death shocked the motorsport world and triggered a thorough review of safety measures in Formula 1.

Senna's accident, coupled with the death of Austrian driver Roland Ratzenberger during the same race weekend, led to a series of significant changes in circuit safety, car designs, and medical teams present at Formula 1 races.

Ayrton Senna's legacy continues to live on in the memories of fans and in motorsport at large. His tragic death spurred substantial changes in Formula 1 safety, which helped reduce risks and enhance protection for drivers on the track.

Rivalries:

-Alain Prost: Senna and Prost were teammates at McLaren in 1988 and 1989, intensifying their rivalry. The two drivers had several on-track clashes, but the most notorious collision occurred at the 1989 Japanese Grand Prix, where Prost shut the door, causing a crash that led to Senna's disqualification. This rivalry reached its zenith in 1990 when Senna deliberately collided with Prost at the first corner of the Japanese Grand Prix, clinching the world championship in the process.

-Nigel Mansell: Senna also had a few run-ins with British driver Nigel Mansell, notably at the 1991 Spanish Grand Prix. During a fierce battle on the final lap, Senna overtook Mansell in a daring move and won the race.

-Nelson Piquet: Despite being fellow Brazilians, Senna and Piquet had an on-track rivalry. The competition between the two developed during their years in Formula 1, particularly in the 1980s. However, after retiring from racing, Piquet became a close advisor and friend to Senna.

JUAN MANUEL
FANGIO

4

JUAN MANUEL FANGIO.

Nicknamed "El Maestro", he was a prominent Argentine racing driver.

He was born on June 24, 1911, in Balcarce, Argentina, and passed away on July 17, 1995, in Buenos Aires, Argentina.

-Formula 1 Career: He competed in Formula 1 for 8 seasons, in 1950 and 1951, and then from 1953 to 1958. During that period, he drove for teams such as Alfa Romeo, Maserati, Mercedes-Benz, and Ferrari.

-World Championships: He won a total of 5 Formula 1 World Championships, a record that stood for several decades. His championships were won in 1951 (with Alfa Romeo), 1954 and 1955 (with Mercedes-Benz), 1956 (with Ferrari), and 1957 (with Maserati). Fangio held the championship record until it was surpassed by Michael Schumacher in 2003.

-Driving Style and Skills: He was known for his smooth, precise, and strategic driving style. He had a great ability to conserve the tires and the car, which allowed him to maintain a consistent pace and adapt to varying race conditions. His knack for managing the car's resources was key to his success.

-Formula 1 Records: He set several notable records in Formula 1. He was the first driver to achieve 5 world championships and held the record for the highest win percentage in a season until 1988, when it was surpassed by Ayrton Senna.

-Retirement and Legacy: He retired from Formula 1 racing in 1958, having raced in a total of 51 Grand Prix and achieved 24 wins. After his retirement, he remained involved in motorsport as an ambassador and a prominent figure at events and tributes.

Superstitions:

-Number 1: He often preferred to carry the number 1 on his car as the defending champion. During his career in Formula 1, world champions would usually carry the number 1 on their cars instead of their regular numbers.

–Religious Medal: It's known that Fangio carried a religious medal with him during races as a symbol of protection and good luck.

–Mental Focus: He had a very focused mindset and believed in the importance of concentration and positive visualization before and during races. While not considered a superstition in itself, his emphasis on mental preparation and focus resembles the rituals of other drivers.

Accidents:

–German Grand Prix 1952: At the 1952 German Grand Prix, Fangio had an accident when his Maserati lost a rear wheel and crashed into a tree. Fortunately, Fangio was unharmed in the incident.

–French Grand Prix 1956: During the 1956 French Grand Prix at Reims-Gueux, Fangio was involved in a collision with another car early in the race. However, he managed to continue in the race and finished in fourth position.

–Argentinian Grand Prix 1958: In his final Formula 1 race, the 1958 Argentinian Grand Prix, Fangio had an accident on the first lap when he collided with another car. Fortunately, he did not suffer serious injuries and was able to retire from the race.

Rivalries:

–Alberto Ascari: Fangio and Ascari had a friendly and respectful rivalry in the 1950s. Both drivers were considered the best of their time and competed in several memorable races. Ascari won two consecutive championships in 1952 and 1953, while Fangio won five championships in total.

–Stirling Moss: Fangio and Moss formed a particularly intense and thrilling rivalry. They faced off in several exciting races and often exchanged victories. Fangio came to regard Moss as one of his greatest rivals and a highly talented driver.

–Mike Hawthorn: Fangio and Hawthorn also had some on-track disputes. At the 1957 German Grand Prix, Fangio and Hawthorn were involved in an incident that led to Fangio's disqualification. However, despite these conflicts, both drivers also shared moments of mutual respect.

ALAIN PROST

5

ALAIN PROST.

Nicknamed "The Professor", he is a former French racing driver.

He was born on February 24, 1955, in Lorette, France.

-Formula 1 Career: He competed in Formula 1 for 13 seasons, from 1980 to 1991 and then in 1993. During this time, he raced for several prominent teams, including McLaren, Renault, Ferrari, and Williams.

-World Championships: He won a total of 4 Formula 1 World Championships. His titles were achieved in the years 1985, 1986, 1989, and 1993. This tally placed him second in the record for championships won at the time, only behind Juan Manuel Fangio.

-Driving Style and Skills: He was known for his calculated and strategic approach on the track. He had a unique ability to handle and conserve tires, as well as to make tactical decisions during races. He was regarded as a highly intelligent and skilled driver in terms of race management.

-Retirement and Legacy: He retired from Formula 1 racing in 1993, after a successful career that included 51 wins and 33 pole positions in 199 Grand Prix races. After his retirement, he continued to be involved in motorsport as a consultant and team owner.

Superstitions:

-Race Number: It's said that Prost had a preference for certain race numbers. Throughout his career, he mainly used the number 2 and the number 7 on his cars.
The number 2 was associated with his status as the championship runner-up in several seasons, while number 7 was his personal favorite number.

-Visualization and Focus: He was known for his methodical approach and strategic mindset. It's said that he practiced visualization and concentration techniques before races to mentally prepare himself and stay focused on the objective.

Accidents:

-Monaco Grand Prix 1984: During the qualifying for the Monaco Grand Prix, Prost had an accident at the harbor turn while attempting to set a fast lap. Although he was unhurt, the incident affected his starting position in the race.

-Portugal Grand Prix 1988: In this incident, Prost collided with Ayrton Senna at the first turn of the Estoril circuit. The crash resulted in both drivers retiring from the race, leading to a major controversy and tension in their rivalry.

-Japan Grand Prix 1989: This race is remembered for the famous incident between Prost and Senna at the Suzuka circuit chicane. Prost and Senna collided at the first corner following a disputed start, leading to Prost's retirement from the race and Senna's world championship.

-Germany Grand Prix 1990: Prost had an accident in the German Grand Prix when he collided with Nigel Mansell during a fight for position. The incident damaged Prost's car, forcing him to retire from the race.

Rivalries:

-Ayrton Senna: The rivalry between Prost and Ayrton Senna is one of the most famous and controversial in Formula 1 history. Both drivers were teammates at McLaren in 1988 and 1989 and had several confrontations on the track. The rivalry reached its peak at the 1989 Japan Grand Prix, where Senna intentionally collided with Prost at the first corner, leading to the disqualification of both drivers. These incidents further intensified the rivalry between them.

-Nelson Piquet: Prost also had a rivalry with Nelson Piquet, another prominent driver from the 1980s. They competed in different teams and had several encounters on the track. Notably, their rivalry intensified at the 1986 German Grand Prix when Piquet overtook Prost on the last lap to secure the victory.

-Nigel Mansell: Prost and Nigel Mansell also had some notable clashes on the track. At the 1987 Portugal Grand Prix, Prost and Mansell collided while battling for position, resulting in both drivers retiring from the race. Their rivalry persisted for several years, especially when Mansell joined Ferrari in 1989.

NIKI LAUDA

6

NIKI LAUDA.

He was a renowned Austrian racing driver.

He was born on February 22, 1949, in Vienna, Austria, and passed away on May 20, 2019.

-World Championships: He won the Formula 1 world championship three times. His first title came in 1975 with the Ferrari team. However, his most memorable season was in 1976, when he suffered a severe crash at the German Grand Prix and made a swift return to racing, competing against James Hunt in a thrilling championship battle. Lauda eventually secured his second championship in 1977 and temporarily retired from Formula 1 in 1979. He made a comeback in 1982 and clinched his third championship in 1984 with McLaren.

-Driving Style and Skills: He was a highly skilled, disciplined, and methodical driver. His precise driving, ability to stay focused, and tire management gave him a competitive edge on the track. His technical knowledge and adaptability made him a versatile driver capable of competing in various conditions.

-Straightforward Personality: He was known for being forthright and direct in his comments and opinions. He wasn't afraid to voice his thoughts and beliefs, which sometimes stirred controversy and disagreements with other drivers and figures in Formula 1. However, he was also respected for his honesty and no-nonsense approach.

-Leader and Entrepreneur: After retiring from racing, Lauda delved into various businesses related to motorsport and aviation. He founded his own airline, Lauda Air, and served as a Formula 1 consultant and commentator.

Accidents:

-The 1976 German Grand Prix accident: This was the most famous and dramatic accident in Niki Lauda's career. It occurred on August 1, 1976, at the Nürburgring circuit during a qualifying lap. Lauda lost control of his Ferrari on a fast bend and collided with the barriers, causing his car to burst into flames. The driver was trapped inside the burning vehicle for several seconds before other racers could rescue him. Lauda sustained severe burns to his head and much of his body, as well as inhaling toxic smoke. Despite the injuries he endured, he returned to racing just six weeks after the crash.

-The 1977 Canadian Grand Prix accident: This accident took place on October 8, 1977, at the Mosport Park circuit during practice for the Canadian Grand Prix. Niki Lauda lost control of his race car and smashed into the containment wall. Fortunately, he didn't suffer serious injuries this time and walked away unharmed from the crash.

Rivalries:

-James Hunt: Lauda's most famous rivalry was with British driver James Hunt. The two had fierce competition during the 1976 season, which included Lauda's accident at Nürburgring. Despite their on-track rivalry, Lauda and Hunt also had mutual respect off the track. Their story was immortalized in the 2013 movie "Rush."

-Alain Prost: Lauda also had a rivalry with Alain Prost, another legendary Formula 1 driver. Prost and Lauda were teammates at McLaren during the 1984 season. Although they had disagreements and disputes, they also held mutual admiration and worked together to develop the McLaren MP4/2, which was a highly successful car.

-Carlos Reutemann: Lauda and the Argentine driver Carlos Reutemann had several on-track clashes during the 1975 season. Lauda, driving for Ferrari, and Reutemann, driving for Brabham, battled for the championship that year.
While there was tension between them, there was also mutual respect and acknowledgment of each other's driving skills.

SEBASTIAN VETTEL

7

SEBASTIAN VETTEL.

He is a renowned racing driver born on July 3, 1987, in Heppenheim, Germany.

-Formula 1 Career: He made his Formula 1 debut in 2007 with the BMW Sauber team as a replacement driver. He later joined Toro Rosso in 2008 and achieved his first win at the Italian Grand Prix, becoming the youngest driver to win a Formula 1 race. In 2009, he moved to Red Bull Racing, where he reached the peak of his career.

-World Championships: He clinched four consecutive Formula 1 world titles with Red Bull Racing in the years 2010, 2011, 2012, and 2013. During these years, he demonstrated impressive dominance by winning a total of 39 races and setting several records. His four straight championships place him in an elite group of drivers to achieve such a feat.

-Move to Ferrari: In 2015, Vettel joined the Ferrari team, one of the most iconic stables in Formula 1. During his time with Ferrari, Vettel secured wins and showed solid performance but couldn't clinch a world championship. His stint at Ferrari spanned from 2015 to the end of the 2020 season.

-Aston Martin: Starting from the 2021 season, Sebastian Vettel joined the Aston Martin Cognizant Formula One Team. This partnership marks a new phase in his career, and Vettel is expected to bring his expertise and talent to the team.

-Driving Characteristics and Style: He's known for his methodical approach and ability to stay calm under pressure. He has an excellent knack for qualifying well on the grid and is considered a tactical driver. Additionally, Vettel is known for his dedication and teamwork, being respected by both his teammates and rivals on the track.

-Other Honors: Besides his world championships, Vettel has received several awards and honors throughout his career, including the Laureus Sportsman of the Year award in 2014.

Superstitions:

-Helmet Number: Throughout his career, Vettel has sported the helmet number "5" as a tribute to his childhood idol, Michael Schumacher, who also used to carry that number. Even when required to use other numbers due to FIA regulations, he's kept the "5" as a sticker on his helmet.

-Entering the car from the left side: He has a habit of entering his race car from the left side before every race. This has become somewhat of a ritual for him, and he does it consistently.

-Race Start: Before the start of each race, Vettel has a ritual of tapping his seat belt three times while seated in his car. This gesture is seen as part of his mental focus and preparation for the competition.

-Lucky Coin: On some occasions, Vettel has carried a lucky coin in his pocket during races. The coin might be a personal item or something lent by someone close to him. This superstition is associated with attracting good luck and maintaining focus during competition.

Accidents:

-Turkey Grand Prix 2010: During the race in Istanbul, Vettel was leading the pack when he had an incident with his Red Bull teammate, Mark Webber. Both drivers collided while vying for position, resulting in Vettel's retirement and significant damage to his car.

-Belgium Grand Prix 2010: At Spa-Francorchamps, Vettel got involved in a first-lap incident with Jenson Button and Fernando Alonso. The collision led to Vettel's retirement and other drivers' withdrawal.

-Italy Grand Prix 2011: During the race in Monza, Vettel was hit by McLaren's driver, Lewis Hamilton, on the first lap. The impact damaged Vettel's rear wing, forcing him into an early pit stop. Though he managed to continue the race, he finished in fourth position.

-Germany Grand Prix 2012: At Hockenheim, Vettel had a crash during the formation lap when he lost control of his car and hit the barrier. The incident damaged his steering, and he had to retire even before the race began.

Rivalries:

-Mark Webber: Vettel and his Red Bull Racing teammate, Mark Webber, shared a tense relationship and on-track rivalry. There were several incidents and clashes between the two, notably in the 2010 Turkey Grand Prix where they collided while vying for position.

-Fernando Alonso: Vettel and Spanish driver Fernando Alonso had an intense rivalry during the years when both were competing for world championships. In 2010 and 2012, Alonso and Vettel contested the title down to the last race of the season. Their on-track battles produced thrilling and tense moments.

-Lewis Hamilton: As Lewis Hamilton and Sebastian Vettel became dominant drivers in Formula 1, a rivalry emerged between them. They competed for world championships and were involved in several on-track duels. In some instances, their disputes led to contact and tension, as in the 2017 Azerbaijan Grand Prix.

-Max Verstappen: The rivalry between Sebastian Vettel and Max Verstappen has gained prominence in recent years. Verstappen, one of the youngest and most talented drivers in Formula 1, has had close encounters with Vettel on the track. They've showcased moments of racing battles and overtaking, leading to a growing rivalry.

FERNANDO ALONSO

8

FERNANDO ALONSO.

He is a prominent racing driver born on July 29, 1981, in Oviedo, Spain.

-Formula 1 Career: He made his Formula 1 debut in 2001 with the Minardi team. He quickly showcased his talent and passion for racing, and by 2003, he joined the Renault team, where he achieved his greatest successes in the category.

-World Championships: He has won the Formula 1 world championship twice. His first victory came in 2005, making him the youngest champion in Formula 1 history at that time. He secured the title again the following year, in 2006, solidifying his status as one of the top drivers of his era.

-Teams he has raced for: Throughout his Formula 1 career, Alonso has raced for several teams. In addition to Minardi and Renault, he has driven for McLaren (on two separate stints: 2007 and 2015-2018) and Alpine F1 Team (previously Renault, since 2021).

-Other Competitions: Beyond Formula 1, Alonso has ventured into other motorsport disciplines. He has taken part in endurance races like the 24 Hours of Le Mans, which he won in 2018 and 2019, and the FIA World Endurance Championship. He also competed in the famed Dakar Rally in 2020.

-Driving Characteristics and Style: He is known for his ability to extract the utmost performance from his car and being an incredibly well-rounded driver. He stands out for his aggressiveness, overtaking skill, and the ability to swiftly adapt to various track conditions. His focus and determination have led him to achieve great accomplishments in motorsport.

-Return to Formula 1: After a temporary retirement from Formula 1 at the end of the 2018 season, Alonso returned to the category in 2021 with the Alpine team. His comeback was highly anticipated by fans, and he continues to compete to this day.

Superstitions:

-Lucky Charm: He often carries a lucky charm with him during races. It was a horseshoe-shaped piece of metal that he believed provided him with good luck and protection during competitions. This charm was typically kept in his pocket or hung in his race car.

-Competition Number: Throughout his career, Fernando Alonso has raced with various competition numbers. During his time at Renault and for his two world championships, Alonso used the number "5" on his race car. However, when he joined the McLaren team in 2007, he adopted the number "1" as the defending champion. Subsequently, he has used different numbers in different seasons, depending on regulations and team decisions.

Accidents:

-Belgian Grand Prix 2012: During the first lap of the race at Spa-Francorchamps, Alonso was involved in a massive accident that occurred at the La Source turn. Romain Grosjean, the Lotus driver, touched another car and was launched into Alonso's McLaren, causing a chain-reaction crash. Fortunately, Alonso emerged unscathed, but the incident resulted in several cars being damaged and having to retire.

-Preseason Test in Barcelona 2015: Alonso had an accident during the preseason training at the Circuit de Barcelona-Catalunya. He lost control of his McLaren at turn 3 and crashed into the wall at high speed. He was taken to the hospital and was diagnosed with a concussion. As a result, he missed the Australian Grand Prix that year.

-Australian Grand Prix 2016: During the first lap of the race in Melbourne, Alonso was involved in a multi-car accident. Haas driver, Esteban Gutiérrez, lost control of his car and collided with Alonso's McLaren, sending it into the barriers. Thankfully, Alonso walked away unhurt, but the crash ended his race prematurely.

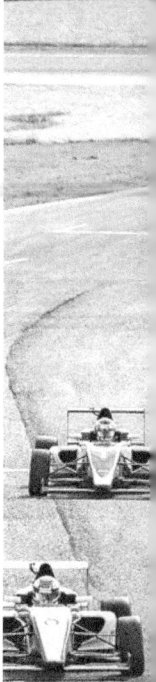

–Belgian Grand Prix 2018: On the first lap of the race at Spa-Francorchamps, Alonso was involved in a crash at the La Source turn. Nico Hülkenberg, a Renault driver, tried to overtake Alonso on the outside of the corner and ended up colliding with his McLaren. The incident resulted in Alonso's car flying over Charles Leclerc's Sauber. Fortunately, none of the drivers were injured.

Rivalries:

–Lewis Hamilton: Alonso and Lewis Hamilton were teammates at McLaren in the 2007 season. Their relationship became strained due to the intense competition between them and internal conflicts within the team. There were disputes over equal treatment and team strategies, leading to an intense rivalry both on and off the track.

–Sebastian Vettel: Alonso and Sebastian Vettel became direct rivals in the fight for the world championship across several seasons. Particularly in 2010 and 2012, Alonso and Vettel battled for the title down to the last race. Their on-track battles, as well as their comments off the track, created an exciting rivalry between two of the best drivers of their time.

–Mark Webber: During his time at the Renault team, Alonso had a rivalry with Mark Webber, who was also a Formula 1 driver. There were several incidents and clashes between them on the track, which led to competitive tension and friction.

–Felipe Massa: Alonso and Felipe Massa were teammates at Ferrari for several seasons. While there wasn't an intense rivalry between them, there were tense situations, especially in the 2010 season when Alonso was fighting for the championship and Massa received team orders to aid his teammate.

NELSON PIQUET SOUTO MAIOR

9

NELSON PIQUET SOUTO MAIOR.

Commonly known as Nelson Piquet, he is a Brazilian racing driver born on August 17, 1952, in Rio de Janeiro, Brazil.

He is considered one of the most successful and talented Formula 1 drivers of the 1980s.

-Formula 1 Career: He made his Formula 1 debut in 1978 with the Ensign team and then raced for Brabham and Williams. He won his first world championship in 1981 with Brabham, repeating the feat in 1983 and 1987 with the same team. In total, he participated in 204 Grand Prix races and won 23 races during his Formula 1 career.

-Driving Style and Abilities: He was known for his smooth and technical driving style. He was a smart and strategic driver who maximized his technical knowledge and his ability to manage tires. He was also regarded as a specialist in car setup and tuning, allowing him to get the most performance out of his machine.

-World Titles: He won three Formula 1 world championships in his career. He secured his first title in 1981 with Brabham, beating Carlos Reutemann and Alan Jones. He repeated the success in 1983, defeating Alain Prost and René Arnoux, and in 1987, besting Nigel Mansell and Ayrton Senna.

-Retirement and Legacy: He retired from Formula 1 in 1991, after racing his final season with the Benetton team. Although his Formula 1 career came to an end, his legacy as one of the most successful drivers of his generation endures. His influence and contributions to Brazilian and international motorsport are recognized and appreciated to this day.

Accidents:

-German Grand Prix 1977: In his rookie season in Formula 1 with the Ensign team, Piquet suffered a severe accident at the Nürburgring Nordschleife. His car crashed into barriers at the famous Pflanzgarten turn, resulting in injuries to his left leg. The accident sidelined him for several races.

-Brazilian Grand Prix 1982: On the first lap of the race in Jacarepaguá, Piquet was involved in a multiple car accident. His Brabham collided with Alain Prost's Renault and Didier Pironi's car, leading to several cars being affected. Fortunately, Piquet did not suffer severe injuries in the incident.

-San Marino Grand Prix 1987: During qualifying practice, Piquet had an accident at the Tamburello corner. He lost control of his Brabham and violently crashed into the barrier, destroying his car. Fortunately, Piquet emerged unharmed from the accident.

-Preseason Test in Rio de Janeiro 1988: Piquet had an accident during the preseason practice at the Nelson Piquet International Autodrome. His Lotus went off the track and collided with a wall, suffering injuries to his hands and back. The accident kept him out of competition for several races.

Rivalries:

-Nigel Mansell: The rivalry between Nelson Piquet and Nigel Mansell was one of the most notable in the 1980s. Both were teammates at Williams during the 1986 and 1987 seasons. Their relationship became strained due to the championship fight and internal team disputes. Despite their differences, they also had moments of mutual respect and collaboration.

-Alain Prost: Piquet also had a rivalry with Alain Prost, another great Formula 1 driver of the same era. Both fought intensely for world championships in several seasons. Their rivalry was heightened by on-track clashes and differences in driving approach and personality.

-Ayrton Senna: While it cannot be said that Piquet and Senna had an openly hostile rivalry, there was intense competition between them. Both Brazilian drivers were successful in Formula 1 and vied for the status of Brazil's number one driver. However, they also supported and collaborated with each other at times, especially in international competitions.

JACKIE STEWART

10

JACKIE STEWART.

His full name is Sir John Young "Jackie" Stewart.

He is a Scottish racing driver born on June 11, 1939, in Dumbarton, Scotland.

–Formula 1 Career: He competed in Formula 1 between 1965 and 1973. Throughout his career, he raced for the BRM (British Racing Motors) and Tyrrell teams. He contested a total of 99 Grand Prix races, claiming 27 wins, 43 podiums, and 17 pole positions.

–World Championships: He won three Formula 1 World Championships in 1969, 1971, and 1973. He became the first driver to win the Formula 1 championship with the Tyrrell team, a private British outfit, in 1969. His titles were marked by his consistency and his focus on safety and race conditions improvements.

–Safety Advocacy: He is renowned for his pioneering work on enhancing safety in motorsport. After witnessing several severe accidents and losing friends on the track, he became an unwavering advocate for racing safety. His activism led to the implementation of life-saving safety measures, like the enhancement of tracks, the introduction of safer helmets and suits, and the promotion of higher safety standards in the sport.

–Driving Style and Abilities: He was known for his calculated and methodical approach to racing. A technical and cunning driver, he was acclaimed for his ability to manage tires and car resources. Besides his driving talent, he was also recognized for his capability to establish a strong and productive bond with his team, collaboratively working to boost the car's performance and reliability.

–Retirement and Legacy: He retired from Formula 1 at the end of the 1973 season, after securing his third world title. Since his retirement, he has remained active in the motorsport world and in promoting safety within the sport. His contribution to motorsport and his legacy as a champion and safety advocate are widely recognized and respected.

Accidents:

-Belgian Grand Prix 1966: In this race, held at the Spa-Francorchamps circuit, Stewart was involved in a serious accident resulting in the death of Italian driver Lorenzo Bandini. Bandini crashed into the barriers and his car caught fire. Stewart and other drivers tried to assist, but they couldn't save Bandini. This accident had a significant impact on Stewart and contributed to his subsequent advocacy for safety in motorsport.

-French Grand Prix 1967: During the race at the Rouen-Les-Essarts circuit, Stewart had an accident on the first lap. His BRM collided with Mike Spence's Lotus, who lost his life in the incident. Stewart escaped unharmed, but the accident had an emotional impact on him.

-Italian Grand Prix 1973: In Monza, during race practice, Stewart had a serious crash. His Tyrrell car crashed into a safety barrier due to a suspension issue. Fortunately, he managed to get out of the car on his own, but the accident led him to decide to retire from Formula 1 at the end of the season.

Rivalries:

-Jim Clark: Though they were close friends off the track, Stewart and Jim Clark, another legendary Scottish driver, had a friendly rivalry in competition. Both raced during the same era and on different teams. As Stewart began to shine, he became a strong competitor for Clark, and their rivalry was evident on the track.

-Graham Hill: Stewart and Graham Hill, another successful British driver, had a competitive rivalry in Formula 1. Both drivers were world champions and raced on different teams. Their rivalry was based on their battle for titles and their desire to outdo each other on the track.

-Jochen Rindt: Stewart and Jochen Rindt, an Austrian driver, had a competitive rivalry in Formula 1. Both were talented drivers and fought for the championship across several seasons. Their rivalry intensified when Rindt became the first driver to posthumously win the Formula 1 world championship in 1970, following his tragic death in a Monza accident.

JIM CLARK

11

JIM CLARK.

His full name is James Clark Jr., and he was a prominent Scottish racing driver born on March 4, 1936, in Kilmany, Scotland.

-Formula 1 Career: He competed in Formula 1 from 1960 to 1968. Throughout his career, he raced for the Lotus team and was widely recognized as the star driver of the squad. He participated in a total of 73 Grand Prix races, securing 25 wins, 32 podium finishes, and 33 pole positions.

-World Championships: He won the Formula 1 World Championship twice, in 1963 and 1965. During these seasons, he showcased his exceptional driving skills and dominated various circuits worldwide. He was the first British driver to achieve two Formula 1 World Championships.

-Driving Style and Abilities: He was known for his smooth and precise driving style. He had a natural ability to quickly adapt to changing track conditions, and his prowess on fast and technical circuits was astounding. He was considered a master in the counter-steering technique and had an exceptional ability to sense and control his car's traction.

-Achievements in Other Categories: Apart from his success in Formula 1, Clark also had an illustrious career in other motor racing categories. He won the Indianapolis 500 in 1965, becoming the first foreign driver to achieve this feat since 1916. He also excelled in touring car races and the 24 Hours of Le Mans.

Accidents:

-Italian Grand Prix 1961: In this race, Clark had a severe accident at the Monza circuit. His Lotus collided with Wolfgang von Trips' Ferrari, leading to the death of von Trips and several spectators. Clark escaped unharmed from the accident.

-**Belgian Grand Prix 1962**: During the race at the Spa-Francorchamps circuit, Clark was involved in an accident on the first lap. His Lotus collided with Trevor Taylor's Lotus, but both drivers emerged unscathed.

-**Mexican Grand Prix 1963**: In this race, Clark had an accident on the first lap due to an issue with his car. His Lotus went off the track and crashed into a ditch. Fortunately, Clark was unharmed in the incident.

-**Italian Grand Prix 1967**: During the race at the Monza circuit, Clark had an accident on the second lap. His Lotus went off the track and collided with a barrier. Regrettably, the accident resulted in the death of a rescue team member who was near the track at that moment.

-**Tragic Death**: Jim Clark's racing career was tragically cut short on April 7, 1968, when he suffered a fatal accident during a Formula 2 race in Hockenheim, Germany. His untimely death shocked the motorsport world and left a lasting legacy.

Rivalries:

Jim Clark, being one of the most successful Formula 1 drivers of his time, didn't have notable rivalries with other drivers on the track.

Despite his racing success and dominance, Clark was known to be a kind, respectful driver and was greatly admired by both his fellow drivers and fans.

However, one can mention a friendly rivalry that existed between Clark and his Lotus teammate, Graham Hill.

Both drivers were supremely talented and raced together for the Lotus team for several seasons.

While there wasn't fierce rivalry, they challenged each other and vied for supremacy on the track, leading to some thrilling duels between them.

Outside of competition, Clark was known for his calm and modest personality, and he got along well with most of the drivers of his era.

He was respected and admired for his driving ability and his focus on technical perfection.

His kindness and friendly demeanor allowed him to forge positive relationships with other drivers rather than intense rivalries.

MIKA HÄKKINEN

12

MIKA HÄKKINEN.

His full name is Mika Pauli Häkkinen, and he is a retired Finnish racing driver born on September 28, 1968, in Vantaa, Finland.

-Formula 1 Career: He competed in Formula 1 from 1991 to 2001. Throughout his career, he drove for the Lotus and McLaren teams. He raced in a total of 161 Grands Prix, claiming 20 victories, 51 podium finishes, and 26 pole positions.

-World Championships: He won the Formula 1 World Championship on two consecutive occasions, in 1998 and 1999. During these seasons, he displayed his prowess behind the wheel and his ability to compete under challenging conditions. He overcame notable rivals like Michael Schumacher to clinch the championships.

-Driving Style and Abilities: He was known for his smooth and precise driving style. He had a great ability to control the car under high-pressure situations and was especially skilled in wet conditions. Additionally, he was considered an overtaking expert and displayed immense determination on track.

-Retirement and Later Life: He retired from Formula 1 at the end of the 2001 season. After his retirement, he remained active in the motorsport world, participating in various competitions and events. He also became an ambassador for automotive brands and worked as a television commentator.

Accidents:

-1995 Australian Grand Prix: He suffered a severe accident during a qualifying session at the Adelaide circuit. His McLaren experienced a failure in the right rear tire, causing him to lose control and violently crash into the wall. The accident left Häkkinen unconscious and with serious injuries, but fortunately, he fully recovered.

-1999 German Grand Prix: During the race at the Nürburgring circuit, Häkkinen had an accident on lap 22. He collided with Jarno Trulli's Williams while trying to overtake him. The crash damaged the rear suspension of his McLaren, forcing him to retire from the race.

-2001 Australian Grand Prix: On the first lap of the race at the Melbourne circuit, Häkkinen had a collision with Jacques Villeneuve's BAR. Both cars sustained significant damage and had to retire from the race.

Rivalries:

-Michael Schumacher: Häkkinen's most notable rivalry was with Michael Schumacher. Both drivers competed during the same era and faced off over several seasons for the world championships. Specifically, the 1998 and 1999 seasons saw intense competition between Häkkinen in McLaren and Schumacher in Ferrari. The two drivers battled for the title in thrilling races and track duels, adding excitement and competition to Formula 1 at that time.

-David Coulthard: While competing for the McLaren team, Häkkinen had David Coulthard as his teammate for several seasons. While there were no intense rivalries between them, they had some on-track clashes while competing for supremacy within the team. However, they maintained a professional and respectful relationship off the track.

NIGEL MANSELL

13

NIGEL MANSELL.

Whose full name is Nigel Ernest James Mansell, is a former British racing driver born on August 8, 1953, in Upton-upon-Severn, Worcestershire, England.

He is considered one of the most notable and popular Formula 1 drivers in the 1980s and early 1990s.

-Formula 1 Career: He competed in Formula 1 between 1980 and 1995, racing for the Lotus, Williams, and McLaren teams. He competed in a total of 187 Grand Prix races and secured 31 victories, 59 podiums, and 32 pole positions.

-World Championship: He won the Formula 1 World Championship in 1992 with the Williams-Renault team. This season was his most successful as he clinched nine races and became the first British driver to win the championship in over 15 years.

-Driving Style and Abilities: He was known for his aggressive and energetic driving style. He was famous for his determination and his ability to overtake other drivers in challenging situations. He was also renowned for his bravery on the track and his skill to push the car to its limits.

-Records and Achievements: He set several records and milestones throughout his career. He was the first driver to break the 180 mph (290 km/h) barrier in Formula 1 qualifying and also set the record for the most pole positions in a season with 14 in 1992. Moreover, he is one of the most successful drivers in Formula 1 history in terms of victories and podiums. After retiring from Formula 1, Mansell ventured into other racing categories, like the IndyCar Series, where he also found success and clinched the championship in 1993.

Superstitions:

-Yellow Helmet: He had the superstition of wearing a yellow helmet for much of his Formula 1 career. The yellow color became his trademark, and many identified him by it. It is said that this superstition originated when Mansell switched to a yellow helmet in 1984 and performed exceptionally well on the track, prompting him to continue using it.

-Coins in Shoes: It's rumored that Mansell used to place coins in his shoes before getting into the race car. This was believed to be part of a ritual to bring good luck and protection during races.

-Sitting on the Right in the Car: Mansell preferred to sit on the right side of the race car during journeys to and from circuits. It is believed that this was due to a personal superstition, giving him a sense of comfort and balance before racing.

Accidents:

-Australian Grand Prix 1984: He had a severe crash at the Adelaide circuit. His car violently hit the barrier wall, resulting in a fractured spine. The accident temporarily paralyzed him, requiring a long recovery period before he could return to racing.

-Japanese Grand Prix 1987: During qualifying at the Suzuka circuit, Mansell had a crash in the famous 130R corner. He lost control of his car and slammed into the protective barrier. The crash seriously damaged his Williams, and although he didn't sustain severe injuries, he had to withdraw from the race.

-Brazilian Grand Prix 1989: On lap 56 of the race at the Jacarepaguá circuit, Mansell was involved in an accident with Ayrton Senna. The two drivers collided when Senna tried to overtake Mansell. The incident damaged both of their cars, forcing them to retire from the race.

Rivalries:

-Ayrton Senna: Mansell and Senna had several on-track confrontations and a fierce rivalry. Both were exceptionally talented and aggressive drivers, and their competitiveness often led them to have thrilling battles. Notably, the incident at the 1989 Japanese Grand Prix, where they collided, led to tensions between them.

-Alain Prost: Mansell and Prost also had a significant rivalry. They raced for different teams but clashed on track on several occasions. In the 1986 season, Mansell was with Williams and Prost with McLaren, and they had numerous battles where they swapped positions and had tense moments.

-Nelson Piquet: Mansell and Piquet were teammates at Williams for some seasons, but they also had a rivalry. Piquet was an experienced and successful driver, and his relationship with Mansell was sometimes tense. They competed for supremacy within the team and often had clashes of personalities.

JUAN PABLO MONTOYA

14

JUAN PABLO MONTOYA.

He is a renowned Colombian racing driver.

He was born on September 20, 1975, in Bogotá, Colombia.

Montoya has competed in a variety of motorsport disciplines, including Formula 1, NASCAR, and endurance racing.

He began his career in karting in Colombia, where he quickly demonstrated his talent and skills.

He then moved to Europe to compete in single-seater categories, and in 1997 he joined the Williams Formula 1 team as a test driver.

The following year, in 1998, he became a full-time driver for Williams, where he secured his first victory at the Italian Grand Prix that same year.

Montoya impressed many with his aggressive driving style and sheer speed.

In 2001, Montoya moved to compete in CART (now known as IndyCar) in the United States, where he quickly stood out.

He won the prestigious Indianapolis 500 in his first attempt in 2000, becoming the first Formula 1 driver to achieve this since 1966.

He also won the CART championship in 1999 and secured numerous victories throughout his career in the United States.

After his stint in CART, Montoya returned to Formula 1 in 2001 as a driver for BMW Williams.

During his time in Formula 1, Montoya proved to be a fast and competitive driver, winning seven Grand Prix races and achieving multiple pole positions.

However, he also had some controversial on-track incidents and faced challenges adapting to regulatory changes in the category.

In 2006, Montoya surprised many by announcing his departure from Formula 1 and his move to NASCAR in the United States.

He competed in the premier NASCAR Cup Series for several years, achieving multiple victories and showcasing his versatility as a driver.

In recent years, Montoya has focused his career on endurance racing. He has competed in events such as the 24 Hours of Le Mans, the 24 Hours of Daytona, and the 12 Hours of Sebring, among others.

Montoya has secured notable victories in these races, including two wins in the 24 Hours of Daytona in 2007 and 2008.

Accidents:

-Monaco Grand Prix 2004: While leading the Formula 1 race on lap 48, Montoya lost control of his car at the Loews corner and collided with a crane parked on the track. Fortunately, he didn't suffer severe injuries but had to retire from the race.

-United States Grand Prix 2005: During the warm-up lap before the race, Montoya went off the track and crashed violently into a safety barrier at turn 13 of the Indianapolis circuit. The crash was caused by a suspension failure in his car. Montoya suffered a concussion and had to miss several races while recovering.

-Brickyard 400, 2007: Competing in the NASCAR Cup Series, Montoya was involved in a massive crash at the Indianapolis Motor Speedway. During a yellow flag, several cars piled up on the back straight, and Montoya couldn't avoid the collision, resulting in a rollover and significant damage to his car.

Rivalries:

-Rivalry with Michael Schumacher: During his time in Formula 1, Montoya had several confrontations with Michael Schumacher, who at the time was considered one of the top drivers in the category. Their rivalry escalated at the 2003 United States Grand Prix when Montoya and Schumacher had an on-track incident resulting in both drivers retiring from the race.

-Rivalry with Lewis Hamilton: Upon his return to Formula 1 in 2011 with the Williams team, Montoya had some clashes with Lewis Hamilton, who was then racing for McLaren. At the 2011 European Grand Prix, Montoya and Hamilton had an on-track incident that led to both drivers retiring from the race.

-Rivalry with Tony Stewart: During his time in NASCAR, Montoya had a rivalry with Tony Stewart, a driver and team owner. The rivalry intensified in oval races, where both drivers were involved in incidents and had on-track skirmishes.

KIMI
RÄIKKÖNEN

15

KIMI RÄIKKÖNEN.

Born on October 17, 1979, in Espoo, Finland, he is a globally recognized Finnish racing driver.

He is known for his aggressive driving style, his skill in changing weather conditions, and his famously reserved personality.

Räikkönen began his career in karting, where he displayed a natural talent for racing.

His progression led him to compete in various single-seater categories before reaching Formula 1.

In 2001, Räikkönen made his Formula 1 debut with the Sauber team.

His impressive performance caught the attention of McLaren, and in 2002 he joined the British team.

During his time with McLaren, Räikkönen won nine Grand Prix races and established himself as one of the fastest and most talented drivers on the grid.

In 2007, Räikkönen joined the Ferrari team, where he reached the pinnacle of his career by winning the Formula 1 World Championship.

In a thrilling battle with Lewis Hamilton and Fernando Alonso, Räikkönen clinched the championship with a victory in the last race of the season.

After his success with Ferrari, Räikkönen took a break from Formula 1 and tried his hand at rallying.

He competed in the FIA World Rally Championship for two years before returning to Formula 1 in 2012 with the Lotus team.

In 2014, Räikkönen rejoined Ferrari, where he raced until the 2021 season.

During his second stint with the Italian team, he achieved several wins and podiums, showcasing his skill and consistency on the track.

In addition to his success in Formula 1, Räikkönen is known for his unique personality and his famous quote "Leave me alone, I know what I'm doing."

His straightforward approach and laid-back attitude have endeared him to fans and earned him the nickname "The Iceman."

In September 2021, Räikkönen announced that he would retire from Formula 1 at the end of the 2021 season.

His career in the category left a lasting legacy and positioned him as one of the most talented and charismatic drivers of his generation.

Superstitions:

-Helmet: He is known to have a special attachment to his racing helmet. He has used the same helmet design for most of his career, with minor variations. This helmet may hold special meaning, or Räikkönen may see it as a kind of lucky charm.

-Racing number: For much of his Formula 1 career, Räikkönen has used the number 7 as his racing number. While not strictly a superstition, some drivers have a preference for certain numbers and may view them as symbols of good luck.

-Underwear: It is said that Räikkönen has a preference for wearing red underwear during races. This could be seen as a small personal superstition related to luck.

Accidents:

-2005 Canadian Grand Prix: He suffered a severe crash during the Formula 1 race at the Circuit Gilles Villeneuve. While battling for the lead, he lost control of his car and collided with the barrier at turn 8, resulting in a rollover. Fortunately, Räikkönen emerged unscathed from the crash.

-2007 Australian Grand Prix: During the Formula 1 qualifying session in Melbourne, Räikkönen had an accident when he lost control of his car at turn 11, crashing into the barrier. The impact damaged his car, preventing him from continuing in the qualifying session.

-2009 Italian Grand Prix: He had a crash during the Formula 1 race at the Monza Circuit. He collided with the tire barriers at the chicane of turn 1 after contact with another car. Thankfully, he didn't sustain any serious injuries.

Rivalries:

-Rivalry with Juan Pablo Montoya: During his time at McLaren, Räikkönen had a rivalry with Colombian driver Juan Pablo Montoya. Both drivers were known for their aggressive driving style and had several on-track confrontations. Notably, there was an incident at the 2005 Monaco Grand Prix, where Montoya tried to overtake Räikkönen and ended up crashing into the wall, resulting in both drivers retiring from the race.

-Rivalry with Lewis Hamilton: During his time at Ferrari, Räikkönen had a rivalry with Lewis Hamilton, especially during the 2008 Formula 1 season. Both drivers were involved in several on-track battles, including an incident at that year's Canadian Grand Prix, where Hamilton crashed into Räikkönen while attempting to overtake him. These confrontations caused tensions between both drivers and their respective teams.

-Rivalry with Sebastian Vettel: During his time at Ferrari, Räikkönen shared the team with Sebastian Vettel, leading to occasional internal rivalry. Both drivers were vying for supremacy within the team and on the track and had some clashes in various races. However, there were also moments of cooperation and mutual respect between them.

JAMES HUNT

16

JAMES HUNT.

Born on August 29, 1947, in Belmont, United Kingdom, he was a British racing driver known for his talent on the track, charismatic personality, and extravagant lifestyle.

He is best known for winning the Formula 1 World Championship in 1976 in an intense battle with Niki Lauda.

Hunt began his racing career competing in various single-seater categories before making his way to Formula 1.

He made his Formula 1 debut in 1973 with the Hesketh Racing team and, despite having a less competitive car initially, showcased his talent by securing good results and catching the attention of the bigger teams.

In 1976, Hunt joined the McLaren team and took part in one of the most thrilling and dramatic seasons in Formula 1 history.

His main rival was Niki Lauda, the Austrian driver for Ferrari. During the German Grand Prix at the Nürburgring circuit, Lauda suffered a horrendous accident that left him with severe burns and injuries.

Despite his injuries, Lauda made a swift return to racing, and the championship battle intensified even further.

The 1976 season reached its climax at the final race in Japan, where Hunt needed to finish at least in third place to clinch the championship.

Despite challenging weather conditions, Hunt pushed hard and managed to finish in third place, allowing him to edge out Lauda by a single point and claim the Formula 1 World Championship title.

After his successful season, Hunt continued to race in Formula 1 until 1979 but never achieved the same level of success again.

He retired from professional racing and transitioned to television commentary, where he shared his insights and perspectives on the races with audiences.

James Hunt is remembered not just for his achievements on the track, but also for his lifestyle off it.

He was known for his love of parties, his fondness for women, and his extroverted personality.

His lavish lifestyle and laid-back attitude earned him widespread popularity, making him a sports icon.

Tragically, James Hunt passed away on June 15, 1993, at the age of 45 due to a heart attack.

His legacy as a driver and his unique personality remain etched in motorsport history.

Accidents:

-Accident at the 1973 Monaco Grand Prix: Hunt suffered a serious crash during the Formula 1 race at the Monaco circuit. He collided with the barrier at the Pool corner, resulting in significant damage to his car and ending his race.

-Accident at the 1976 French Grand Prix: During the qualifying session for the Formula 1 race at the Paul Ricard circuit, Hunt had an accident when his car experienced a rear suspension failure. The crash was severe enough that Hunt sustained a leg fracture, sidelining him from several races.

-Accident at the 1976 Italian Grand Prix: In the opening lap of the Formula 1 race at the Monza circuit, Hunt was involved in a multi-car pileup that involved several other drivers. Despite the damage to his car, Hunt managed to continue in the race and finished in third place.

Rivalries:

-Niki Lauda: James Hunt's most famous rivalry was with Austrian driver Niki Lauda. During the 1976 Formula 1 season, both drivers engaged in a fierce battle for the world championship. Their rivalry was further highlighted after Lauda suffered a severe crash at the German Grand Prix, leading to his hospitalization. Even though they had vastly different lifestyles and personalities, their competition on the track and their fight for the title created a thrilling and memorable rivalry.

-Jochen Mass: He also had a rivalry with German driver Jochen Mass. During the 1976 Formula 1 season, Hunt and Mass were teammates at McLaren. Even though Hunt was the more successful driver of the team, tensions arose between them. The rivalry between Hunt and Mass intensified when Mass crashed during the race at the Nürburgring circuit, shortly after Niki Lauda's accident. This sparked criticisms and strains within the team.

-Mario Andretti: While their rivalry was more subdued compared to the ones mentioned above, James Hunt had some clashes with American driver Mario Andretti. Both drivers competed in Formula 1 during the 1970s and had some brushes on the track. While it wasn't an intense rivalry, their racing competition and different driving styles brought about some tension between them.

DAMON HILL

17

DAMON HILL.

Born on September 17, 1960, in Hampstead, London, United Kingdom, Damon Hill is a British racing driver renowned for his successful career in Formula 1.

He is the son of the legendary driver Graham Hill, who was also a Formula 1 world champion.

Hill began his motorsport career in single-seater categories, but it was in Formula 1 where he reached stardom.

He made his Formula 1 debut in 1992 with the Brabham team and subsequently raced for several teams, including Williams, Arrows, Jordan, and Jaguar.

The highlight of Damon Hill's career was his tenure with the Williams team in the 1990s.

In 1993, he was teammates with the legendary Ayrton Senna at Williams and achieved his first win at the Hungarian Grand Prix.

However, it was during the 1996 season when he reached the pinnacle of success by becoming the Formula 1 world champion.

In 1996, Hill clinched the Formula 1 World Championship with Williams-Renault, beating his teammate, Jacques Villeneuve.

It was a thrilling and challenging season, featuring intense on-track battles and remarkable consistency from Hill.

His victory made him the first son of a Formula 1 world champion to win the world title himself.

After his triumph in 1996, Hill continued racing in Formula 1 until 1999, but he did not achieve the same level of success again.

He retired from professional racing and has since been involved in various activities related to the sport, sharing his expertise and experiences in motorsports.

In addition to his Formula 1 career, Damon Hill has also participated in other motorsport competitions, including endurance racing and the single-seater racing series A1 Grand Prix.

Accidents:

-Accident at the 1998 Belgian Grand Prix: During the Formula 1 race at the Spa-Francorchamps circuit, Hill had an accident on the first lap. His car left the track and crashed into the protective barriers, causing significant damage to the vehicle and ending his race.

-Accident at the 1999 German Grand Prix: In the Formula 1 race at the Nürburgring circuit, Hill had an accident on the first lap. His car collided with Ralf Schumacher's, causing severe damage to both vehicles and putting them out of the race.

Rivalries:

-Michael Schumacher: Damon Hill's most notable rivalry was with the German driver Michael Schumacher. Both drivers faced off in an intense battle for the world championship in the 1990s.
In 1994 and 1995, Hill contended with Schumacher for the title, and on both occasions, Schumacher came out on top. Their rivalry reached its zenith in the 1994 season, where a controversial incident in the final race led to a collision between both drivers, consequently taking Hill out of contention for the championship.

-Jacques Villeneuve: Both drivers were teammates at Williams in 1996, and they battled for the world championship during that season. Although Hill ultimately became the champion, the rivalry between him and Villeneuve was intense and played out several times on track.

-David Coulthard: Both drivers clashed on various occasions during their time in Formula 1, especially when Coulthard was a McLaren driver, and Hill was racing for Williams. Their rivalry was largely on sporting terms and on-track competition.

JENSON BUTTON

18

JENSON BUTTON.

Born on January 19, 1980, in Frome, Somerset, United Kingdom, he is a British racing driver.

He is known for his successful career in Formula 1 and for becoming the world champion in 2009.

Button began his motorsport career at a young age and showed exceptional talent in karting.

At 20, he made his Formula 1 debut with the Williams team in 2000.

Although he had a promising start, it was with the BAR Honda team (which later became Honda Racing F1 Team and finally Brawn GP) where he achieved his greatest success.

In 2009, Jenson Button stunned the motorsport world by winning the Formula 1 World Championship with the Brawn GP team.

It was a dominant season for Button, who won six of the first seven races of the year.

His smooth driving style and ability to manage tires were key factors in his success.

That season, Brawn GP also took the Constructors' title, making them one of the most successful teams in Formula 1 history.

Throughout his Formula 1 career, Button raced for several teams, including Williams, Benetton, Renault, BAR Honda, Honda Racing F1 Team, Brawn GP, and McLaren.

In total, he competed in 306 Grand Prix races, achieving 15 victories, 50 podiums, and 8 pole positions.

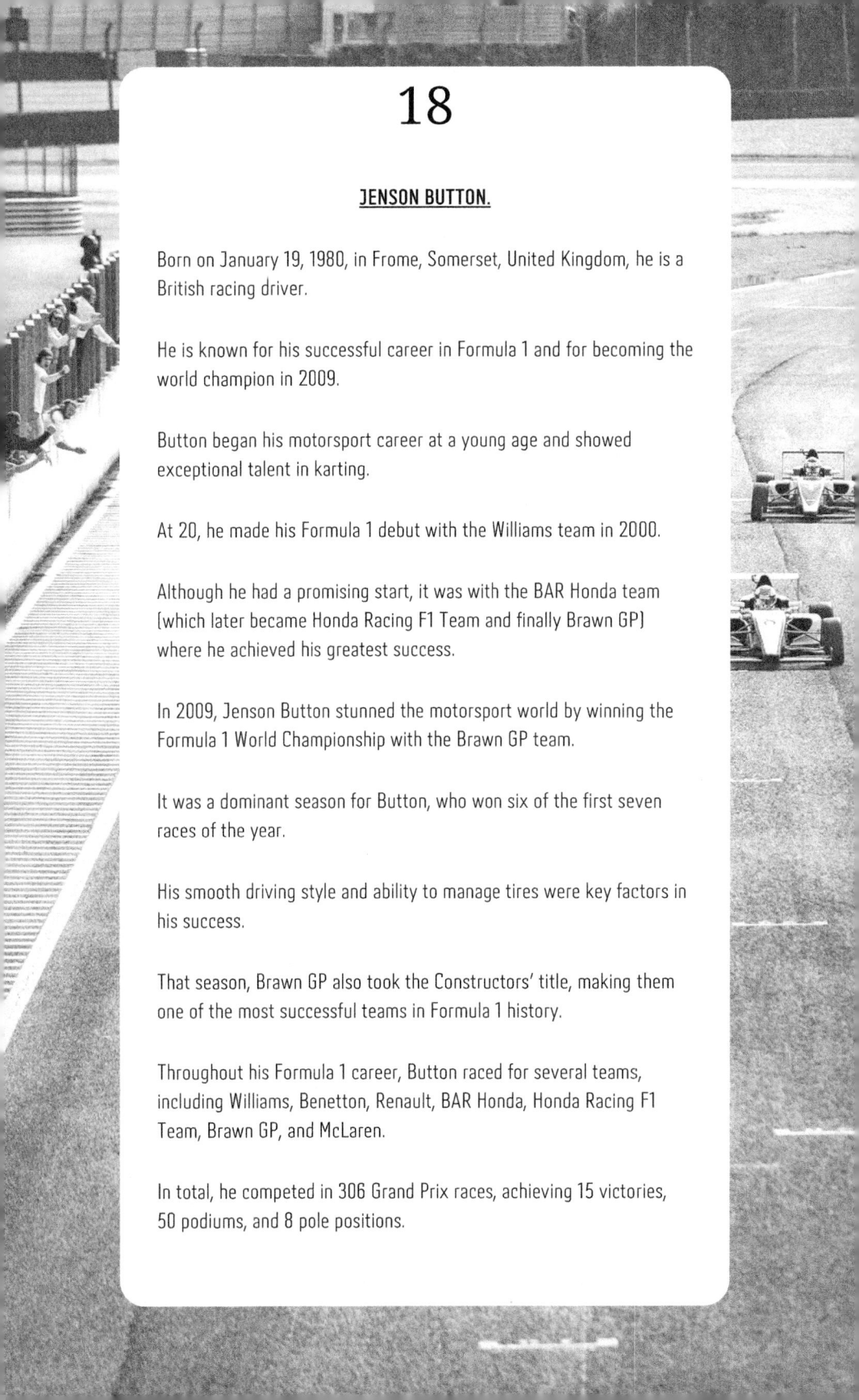

In addition to his world championship, Button was also known for his ability to adapt to different racing conditions and his capability to manage tricky situations on the track.

He was recognized for his methodical approach and his smooth, consistent driving style.

After retiring from Formula 1 at the end of the 2016 season, Button has competed in other races, such as the FIA World Endurance Championship and the Super GT series in Japan.

Off the track, Jenson Button is known for his charisma and friendly demeanor.

Accidents:

-German Grand Prix 2003: In this race, Button, racing for the BAR Honda team, had an accident on lap 27. His car crashed into the wall after losing control due to an issue with the rear suspension.

-Hungarian Grand Prix 2003: In the 2003 season, Button had another accident at the Hungaroring circuit. This time, he was involved in a multi-car collision on the first lap, which caused significant damage to his car, forcing him to retire from the race.

-Canadian Grand Prix 2005: During free practice for this race, Button had a major crash when his car lost control in a turn and collided with the barriers. Fortunately, Button emerged unharmed, but his car sustained considerable damage.

Rivalries:

-Lewis Hamilton: Jenson Button's most notable rivalry was with his McLaren teammate, Lewis Hamilton. Button and Hamilton shared the McLaren garage for three seasons, from 2010 to 2012. Both drivers were talented and competitive, battling fiercely for the top spots in races. Although there was a rivalry on the track, Button and Hamilton maintained a respectful relationship off it.

-Fernando Alonso: Both drivers competed on different teams over several years, and on some occasions, they clashed on the track. The rivalry between Button and Alonso was largely in sporting and competitive terms.

-Sebastian Vettel: Both drivers raced for different teams, but in some races, they found themselves in intense battles. Their rivalry was in sporting terms and reflected the competition on the track.

MAX
VERSTAPPEN

19

MAX VERSTAPPEN.

Born on September 30, 1997, in Hasselt, Belgium, he is a Dutch racing driver.

Verstappen comes from a family with strong ties to motorsport. His father, Jos Verstappen, was also a Formula 1 driver.

Max began his career in karting and quickly demonstrated exceptional talent.

At 16, he became the youngest driver to compete in a Formula 1 Grand Prix when he made his debut with the Toro Rosso team (now known as AlphaTauri) in 2015.

In 2016, Verstappen was promoted to the Red Bull Racing team, where he has achieved notable success.

He has secured multiple wins, podiums, and pole positions throughout his Formula 1 career.

Moreover, he has set several records, including being the youngest driver to win a Formula 1 race (2016 Spanish Grand Prix) and the youngest to secure a pole position (2019 Hungarian Grand Prix).

Max Verstappen is characterized by his aggressive and bold driving style.

He is known for his overtaking skills and determination on the track.

He has shown great car control under challenging conditions and has been at the center of thrilling on-track battles with other drivers.

Throughout his career, Verstappen has developed significant rivalries with other drivers, such as Lewis Hamilton, with whom he has had intense duels on several occasions.

These rivalries have added excitement and drama to Formula 1 races.

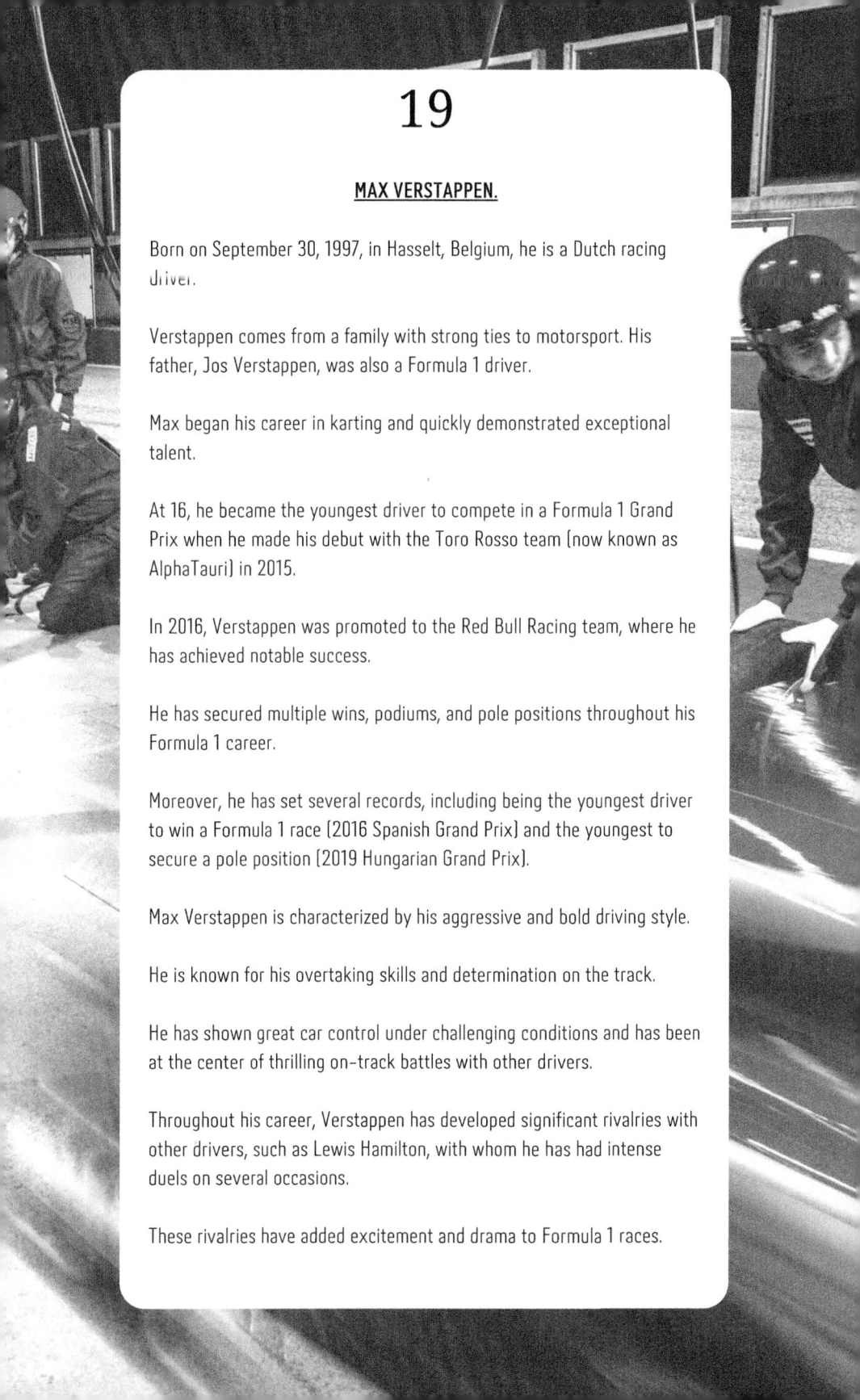

Off the track, Verstappen is regarded as one of the most charismatic and popular drivers in Formula 1.

He is known for his straightforward approach and frankness in expressing his opinions.

He has also been involved in charitable activities and is an ambassador for various brands and organizations.

Despite his youth, Max Verstappen has already made a significant mark on Formula 1, and he is expected to continue being a prominent figure in motorsport in the coming years.

Accidents:

-2015 Monaco Grand Prix: In his debut season in Formula 1 with the Toro Rosso team, Verstappen crashed into the barriers at the famous Sainte Devote corner during the third practice session. The accident severely damaged his car, forcing him to miss both qualifying and the race.

-2016 Belgian Grand Prix: In the first lap of the race, Verstappen was involved in a multi-car accident at the Les Combes corner. He was hit by Kimi Räikkönen's car and got tangled in a collision with several other drivers, leading to his retirement from the race.

-2018 Hungarian Grand Prix: During qualifying, Verstappen lost control of his car at turn 4 and crashed into the barriers. The impact severely damaged his car, preventing him from participating further in the qualifying session. However, he was able to repair his car in time for the race, finishing in fifth place.

Rivalries:

-Lewis Hamilton: The rivalry between Max Verstappen and Lewis Hamilton has been one of the most prominent in recent years. Both drivers have had thrilling duels on the track, with intense battles and daring maneuvers. Their rivalry has evolved due to their struggle for supremacy on the track and the world championship. Their encounters have produced exciting moments and sparked controversial debates among fans.

-Daniel Ricciardo: Before his departure from the Red Bull Racing team, Verstappen had a friendly and competitive rivalry with his teammate, Daniel Ricciardo. Both drivers proved to be highly talented and had thrilling races where they overtook and challenged each other. While there was healthy competition between them, they also had a good relationship off the track.

-Esteban Ocon: At the 2018 Brazilian Grand Prix, Verstappen had a clash with Force India (now Aston Martin) driver Esteban Ocon. After leading most of the race, Verstappen was overtaken by Ocon, who was a lap down. In a subsequent incident, Verstappen and Ocon collided, leading to Verstappen losing the win and sparking a physical confrontation between the two drivers after the race.

DANIEL
RICCIARDO

20

DANIEL RICCIARDO.

Whose full name is Daniel Joseph Ricciardo, is a racing driver born on July 1, 1989, in Perth, Australia.

He is known for his participation in Formula 1 and has raced for several teams throughout his career.

Ricciardo began his journey in karting and then moved up to single-seater categories.

In 2009, he joined the Formula Renault 3.5 Series, where he secured the championship in his rookie season.

This success paved his way into Formula 1.

In 2011, Daniel Ricciardo made his Formula 1 debut with the HRT (Hispania Racing Team).

The following season, he joined Toro Rosso, a sister team to Red Bull Racing. It was with Red Bull where he reached the pinnacle of his career to date.

Ricciardo raced for Red Bull Racing from 2014 to 2018.

During that time, he claimed numerous wins and showcased his skill and prowess as a driver.

His aggressive driving style and ability to overtake in challenging situations made him a fan favorite.

One of Ricciardo's most notable victories came at the 2018 Monaco Grand Prix, where he secured a memorable win despite facing technical issues with his car.

His ability to handle the situation and keep his competitors at bay made it an unforgettable performance.

After his successful stint with Red Bull Racing, in 2019 Ricciardo joined the Renault F1 Team (now known as Alpine F1 Team).

While he hasn't achieved the same results as at Red Bull, he has demonstrated his ability to compete, earning podiums and significant points for his team.

Accidents:

-Australian Grand Prix 2014: On his debut with Red Bull Racing, Ricciardo suffered a crash when he collided with Felipe Massa's car in turn 1 during the first lap of the race.

-Spanish Grand Prix 2016: During the first lap of the race, Ricciardo got involved in an incident at turn 4 with Ferrari driver, Kimi Räikkönen. The collision resulted in both drivers retiring.

-Azerbaijan Grand Prix 2018: Ricciardo was involved in an incident with his Red Bull teammate, Max Verstappen. The two drivers collided while fighting for position, leading to both retiring and internal tension within the team.

Rivalries:

-Max Verstappen: During their time together at Red Bull Racing, Ricciardo and Verstappen had an intense rivalry. Both drivers were teammates and directly competed on the track. The rivalry peaked at the 2018 Azerbaijan Grand Prix when they collided while battling for position.

-Sebastian Vettel: Ricciardo teamed up with Vettel at Red Bull Racing in 2014. During that season, Ricciardo outperformed Vettel on several occasions, even securing three wins while Vettel achieved none. This internal rivalry was the subject of attention and speculation at the time.

-Nico Hülkenberg: Ricciardo and Hülkenberg were teammates at the Renault F1 Team (now known as Alpine F1 Team) in 2019. Both drivers had strong competition on track, challenging each other on various occasions.

CHARLES
LECLERC

21

CHARLES LECLERC.

He is a racing driver from Monaco born on October 16, 1997.

-Early Career: He began his racing career in karting, where he secured numerous national and international titles, including the CIK-FIA World Karting Championship in 2011. He also competed in several single-seater categories, such as Formula Renault 2.0 and the GP3 Series.

-Formula 1 Debut: In 2018, Leclerc made his Formula 1 debut with the Alfa Romeo Sauber team (now known as Alfa Romeo Racing). He impressed with his performance, showing fast and consistent driving skills, leading to his promotion to the Ferrari team the following year.

-Ferrari and Notable Achievements: Since 2019, Leclerc has been a driver for Ferrari in Formula 1. In his first season with Ferrari, he achieved his first Formula 1 victory at the 2019 Belgian Grand Prix. In addition, he secured seven pole positions and several standout performances, challenging seasoned drivers.

-Driving Skills: He is known for his aggressive and brave driving style. He is capable of extracting maximum performance from his car and displays exceptional skills in wet conditions. Moreover, he's regarded as a talented driver in tire management and race strategies.

-Other Achievements: In addition to his success in Formula 1, Leclerc has also participated in endurance races, including the 24 Hours of Le Mans, where he secured a podium in the LMGTE Pro category in 2017.

Accidents:

-Belgian Grand Prix 2018: Leclerc had an accident on the first lap of the race when his Sauber was hit by Fernando Alonso's car at the La Source turn. The incident resulted in a heavy impact and an early retirement for Leclerc from the race.

-German Grand Prix 2019: During qualifying, Leclerc went off the track in wet conditions at turn 16, crashing into the barriers. The accident damaged his Ferrari, forcing him to start the race from the last position.

-**2020 British Grand Prix:** On the first lap of the race, Leclerc had an accident with McLaren's driver, Carlos Sainz Jr., at the Copse corner. The impact severely damaged Leclerc's car and resulted in his retirement from the race.

Rivalries:

-**Sebastian Vettel:** During their time as teammates at Ferrari in the 2019 and 2020 seasons, Leclerc and Sebastian Vettel had moments of rivalry. Both drivers vied for supremacy within the team and found themselves in tense on-track situations, such as collisions and disputes over position. Despite this, they also showed mutual respect and worked together for the benefit of the team.

-**Max Verstappen:** Leclerc and Max Verstappen have been seen as two of Formula 1's rising stars and have had thrilling on-track battles. They have competed for positions in various races and on occasions have had intense, close duels. Their rivalry has been based on their talent and competitiveness, leading to exciting moments for fans.

-**Lewis Hamilton:** While it can't be considered a rivalry in the traditional sense, the relationship between Charles Leclerc and Lewis Hamilton has been interesting to watch. Leclerc has proven to be a driver capable of challenging Hamilton's and Mercedes' dominance in some races, and their on-track battle has been exhilarating. Although they haven't had prolonged rivalries, the competitiveness between them is evident.

SERGIO PÉREZ

22

SERGIO PÉREZ.

Also known as "Checo", he is a Mexican racing driver who competes in Formula 1.

-Formula 1 Career: He made his Formula 1 debut in 2011 with the Sauber team. Since then, he has raced for several teams, including McLaren, Force India/Racing Point, and Red Bull Racing. In 2021, he joined the Red Bull Racing team alongside teammate Max Verstappen.

-Podiums and Wins: Throughout his Formula 1 career, Pérez has achieved multiple podiums and one win. To my current knowledge as of September 2021, he has secured a total of 12 podiums, including a win at the 2020 Sakhir Grand Prix, where he claimed his first Formula 1 victory.

-Consistency and Race Skills: One of Pérez's strengths is his ability to maintain a consistent pace and achieve solid results in complex strategic situations. He has proven to be a skilled driver in wet conditions and is known for his tire management skills, allowing him to achieve good results in tire-degrading races.

-Sponsors and Mexican Support: He has had strong backing from Mexican sponsors throughout his career, which has helped boost his presence in Formula 1. He has also been a popular driver in Mexico and has contributed to the rise in interest and popularity of motorsport in his country.

-Career in Other Championships: Before reaching Formula 1, Pérez competed in various motorsport categories, including Formula BMW, the GP2 Series (now known as Formula 2), and Formula Renault 3.5, where he achieved good results and stood out as a promising driver.

Accidents:

-**Monaco Grand Prix 2011**: In his rookie season in Formula 1 with the Sauber team, Pérez had a crash during the Monaco Grand Prix qualifying session. He lost control of his car at the tunnel turn and collided with the barriers. Fortunately, he didn't suffer any severe injuries.

-**Canadian Grand Prix 2014**: In the 2014 season with the Force India team, Pérez was involved in a crash with his teammate, Nico Hülkenberg, during the 1st lap of the Canadian Grand Prix. Both drivers collided and had to retire from the race.

-**Belgian Grand Prix 2014**: In the same season, Pérez had a crash at the Les Combes turn during the Belgian Grand Prix. His car made contact with Felipe Massa's, which caused Pérez to lose control and hit the barriers. Again, luckily, he did not sustain serious injuries.

-**Russian Grand Prix 2018**: During the first lap of the 2018 Russian Grand Prix, Pérez was involved in a multi-car crash at turn 2. He was hit from behind and was forced to retire from the race due to damage to his car.

Rivalries:

-**Esteban Ocon**: In the 2017 season, Pérez and Esteban Ocon were teammates at Force India. Tensions and conflicts arose between them throughout the season, especially during the Belgian and Italian races. There were several on-track incidents and collisions between the two drivers, leading to a noticeable rivalry.

-**Nico Hülkenberg**: Pérez and Nico Hülkenberg were teammates at Force India during the 2014 and 2015 seasons. While there wasn't an intense rivalry between them, there were some competitive situations where both drivers vied for performance and supremacy within the team.

-**Max Verstappen**: With his move to Red Bull Racing in 2021, Sergio Pérez became teammates with Max Verstappen, one of the most talented and fastest drivers on the Formula 1 grid. While there hasn't been an intense rivalry between them, there is a consistent competition on the track to showcase their skills and achieve strong results.

VALTTERI BOTTAS

23

VALTTERI BOTTAS.

He is a Finnish racing driver who competes in Formula 1.

-Formula 1 Career: He made his Formula 1 debut in 2013 with the Williams team. He spent five seasons with Williams, displaying great potential and achieving good results, including nine podiums and one pole position.

-Mercedes-AMG Petronas Formula One Team: In 2017, Bottas joined the Mercedes team, replacing world champion Nico Rosberg, who retired after winning the title in 2016. Bottas became teammates with Lewis Hamilton, one of the most successful drivers in Formula 1 history.

-Performance and Achievements: Since joining Mercedes, Bottas has proven to be a competitive driver and has been an integral part of the team's successes. He has secured multiple wins, podiums, and pole positions. In his first season with Mercedes in 2017, he finished third in the Drivers' Championship.

-Driving Style: He is known for being a fast and consistent driver. He possesses a smooth technique and is adept at managing tires, which has enabled him to achieve strong results in strategic races.

Accidents:

-Australian Grand Prix 2016: During the season-opening race in Melbourne in 2016, Bottas had a crash at the first corner. He collided with Lewis Hamilton's Williams, resulting in damage to his own car and forcing him to retire from the race.

-Spanish Grand Prix 2019: In the opening lap of the race in Barcelona, Bottas and Charles Leclerc's Ferrari made contact at turn 1. The incident caused damage to Bottas's car and a punctured tire, forcing him into an early pit stop and compromising his performance in the race.

-Azerbaijan Grand Prix 2019: During qualifying, Bottas had an accident at turn 2, damaging his car and causing a red flag that halted the qualifying session. As a result, Bottas started the race from the tenth position.

-Mexico Grand Prix 2019: On the opening lap of the race, Bottas was involved in an incident with Max Verstappen and Lewis Hamilton. All three drivers made contact, and Bottas sustained damage to his car, forcing him into an early pit stop and leaving him to battle the rest of the race from the back of the grid.

Rivalries:

-Lewis Hamilton: As a teammate to Lewis Hamilton at Mercedes, Bottas has had a competitive relationship and a sporting rivalry with the seven-time world champion. Both drivers have battled for top spots in many races and championships, and their on-track duel has been intense. However, they have also demonstrated mutual respect and have worked together for the success of the Mercedes team.

-Sebastian Vettel: During the 2019 season, when Vettel was still racing for Ferrari, there were moments of on-track rivalry between Bottas and Vettel. Both drivers clashed on several occasions, especially during the opening laps of races, where some incidents and tense overtaking situations occurred.

-Max Verstappen: Bottas has had on-track duels with Red Bull driver, Max Verstappen. Both drivers have competed aggressively for positions, especially in the opening laps of races. While no extreme rivalries have emerged, their competition on the track has been intense, and they've had some moments of contact and brushes.

NICO ROSBERG

24

<u>NICO ROSBERG.</u>

He is a retired German racing driver. Born on June 27, 1985, in Wiesbaden, Germany, he is the son of Formula 1 world champion, Keke Rosberg.

Nico Rosberg competed in Formula 1 from 2006 to 2016, reaching the pinnacle of his career by becoming the world champion in 2016 with the Mercedes-AMG Petronas Formula One Team.

–Formula 1 Career: He made his Formula 1 debut in 2006 with the Williams team. Subsequently, in 2010, he joined the Mercedes team and stayed with them until his retirement at the end of the 2016 season. During his F1 career, he achieved a total of 23 wins, 57 podiums, and 30 pole positions.

–2016 World Championship: In the 2016 Formula 1 season, Nico Rosberg delivered an exceptional performance, securing his first and only world championship title. It was a thrilling and closely fought season against his teammate Lewis Hamilton. Rosberg demonstrated great consistency and determination throughout the season to clinch the championship.

–Formula 1 Retirement: After winning the championship in 2016, Nico Rosberg surprised many by announcing his retirement from Formula 1 shortly after. He chose to leave the sport at the height of his career and devote more time to his family and other interests. Since his retirement, he has been engaged in business endeavors and promoting electric mobility.

Accidents:

–Singapore Grand Prix 2008: On the opening lap of the race, Rosberg was involved in a multi-car incident at turn 1. The crash resulted in damage to his car and forced him to retire from the race.

–Monaco Grand Prix 2010: During the qualifying session, Rosberg had an accident at the Casino corner. He lost control of his car and hit the protective barriers, causing significant damage to his car. Thankfully, he did not sustain any serious injuries.

-Belgian Grand Prix 2012: On the first lap of the race, Rosberg was involved in a collision with McLaren driver, Lewis Hamilton. Both cars suffered damage, resulting in Rosberg's retirement from the race.

Rivalries:

-Rivalry with Lewis Hamilton: Rosberg's most well-known rivalry was with his Mercedes teammate, Lewis Hamilton. Both drivers shared the Mercedes garage from 2013 to 2016 and went head-to-head in an intense battle for the world championship. Their rivalry was marked by tense moments on the track, disputes over overtakes, and clashes in team strategies. Although they were teammates, their relationship became increasingly strained and competitive, leading to high-pressure situations and rivalry within the team.

-Rivalry with Sebastian Vettel: Before joining Mercedes, Rosberg raced for the Williams team and, during that time, had a rivalry with Red Bull Racing's driver, Sebastian Vettel. Both drivers were young and talented, competing for podiums and wins on the track. Their rivalry was primarily centered on on-track competition and vying for top positions in races.

JOCHEN RINDT

25

JOCHEN RINDT.

He was an Austrian racing driver born on April 18, 1942, in Mainz, Germany, and tragically died on September 5, 1970, during an accident at the Italian Grand Prix in Monza.

Despite his short life, he left a significant mark on motorsports and became the only driver to win the Formula 1 World Championship posthumously.

-Formula 1 Career: He made his Formula 1 debut in 1964 with the Rob Walker Racing Team. After racing for various teams, including Brabham, Cooper, and Lotus, he joined Team Lotus in 1969 and achieved his greatest success during this stage of his career.

-Driving Style: Rindt was known for his aggressive and brave driving style. He was an extremely fast and bold driver, able to push the limits of his car to the maximum.

-1970 Formula 1 World Championship: In the 1970 season, Rindt delivered an exceptional performance. He won five consecutive races and was leading the championship before his tragic demise at the Italian Grand Prix.

-Legacy: He left a significant legacy in motorsport. He was recognized as a talented and charismatic driver, and his tragic death shocked the motorsport community.

Accidents:

-Monaco Grand Prix 1967: He suffered a severe crash during practice for the Monaco Grand Prix in 1967. He lost control of his car and hit the crash barriers, resulting in significant car damage. Fortunately, Rindt emerged unharmed from the accident.

-Belgian Grand Prix 1968: During the race at Spa-Francorchamps, Rindt had an incident on the first lap. His car got involved in a multi-car collision with other competitors, causing damage to his race car. Despite the crash, Rindt managed to continue in the race and finished in sixth place.

-Italian Grand Prix 1969: In Monza, Rindt suffered an accident during the race. He lost control of his car in the famous Parabolica turn and crashed into the barriers. Fortunately, he emerged unscathed from the accident.

-Canadian Grand Prix 1970: During practice for the race at Mont-Tremblant, Rindt was involved in an accident in the St. Jovite corner. His car flipped over and sustained significant damage. Fortunately, Rindt did not suffer any serious injuries and was able to continue racing.

-Italian Grand Prix 1970: He lost his life in an accident during the qualifying session. This crash, which involved a brake failure in his car, cost him his life, making him the first and only driver to win the Formula 1 World Championship posthumously.

Rivalries:

-Jack Brabham: Rindt raced against three-time world champion Jack Brabham during his early years in Formula 1. Both drivers faced off on several occasions and had thrilling battles on the track.

-Jackie Stewart: Rindt also had competitive encounters with Jackie Stewart, who became one of the most successful drivers of the era. Both drivers showcased their skill and speed in numerous races.

GILLES
VILLENEUVE

26

GILLES VILLENEUVE.

He was a Canadian racing driver born on January 18, 1950, in Saint-Jean-sur-Richelieu, Quebec.

He is considered one of the most iconic and beloved drivers in Formula 1 history due to his aggressive and daring driving style.

-Formula 1 Career: He competed in Formula 1 from 1977 to 1982. He made his debut with the McLaren team in 1977 and subsequently joined the Ferrari team in 1978, where he spent most of his Formula 1 career. He achieved six victories and nine pole positions during his career.

-Driving Style: Gilles Villeneuve was known for his bold and aggressive driving style. He was renowned for his bravery on the track and his ability to pull off spectacular overtakes, even under challenging conditions. His "win or crash" mentality made him one of the most thrilling drivers of his time.

-On-Track Duels: He had several memorable duels on the track, especially with his Ferrari teammate, Didier Pironi. Their rivalry reached its zenith at the 1982 San Marino Grand Prix when Pironi disobeyed team orders and overtook Villeneuve on the final lap to win the race. This incident caused significant tension between the two drivers.

-Legacy and Tragic Death: Sadly, Gilles Villeneuve's career was tragically cut short on May 8, 1982. During the qualifying session for the Belgian Grand Prix in Zolder, Villeneuve collided violently with Jochen Mass's car. The crash was fatal, and Villeneuve lost his life at the age of 32.

-Tributes and Recognitions: Gilles Villeneuve left an indelible mark on the racing world and remains fondly remembered and admired by Formula 1 fans. The Gilles Villeneuve Circuit in Montreal, Canada, is named in honor of his legacy. Additionally, his son, Jacques Villeneuve, followed in his footsteps and became the Formula 1 world champion in 1997.

Accidents:

-South African Grand Prix 1977: In his rookie Formula 1 season with the McLaren team, Villeneuve had an accident at the season's first Grand Prix in Kyalami. He collided with another car and was forced out of the race.

-Canadian Grand Prix 1977: In his home race, Villeneuve crashed on the final lap at the Gilles Villeneuve Circuit. Despite the crash, he managed to cross the finish line in third place.

-Argentine Grand Prix 1979: During qualifying, Villeneuve had an accident which resulted in his car flipping over. Fortunately, he wasn't seriously injured and was able to compete in the race.

-Belgian Grand Prix 1979: In a race marked by adverse weather conditions, Villeneuve crashed on a wet curve. Though he was able to continue, he ultimately had to retire due to damage to his car.

-Italian Grand Prix 1979: In the qualifying session, Villeneuve had an accident at the famous Monza Parabolic curve. The crash was severe enough to damage his car, and he couldn't compete in the race.

Rivalries:

-Didier Pironi: Villeneuve and Pironi were teammates at Ferrari in 1982. The rivalry between the two reached its peak at that year's San Marino Grand Prix. During the race, Pironi disobeyed team orders and overtook Villeneuve on the final lap to claim victory. This incident created significant tension and resentment between the two drivers.

-René Arnoux: Villeneuve and Arnoux had one of the most memorable duels in Formula 1 history. At the 1979 French Grand Prix, the two drivers engaged in an epic battle, executing numerous overtakes and daring maneuvers. Their wheel-to-wheel combat was a highlight of the race and has become one of the most remembered moments in motorsport history.

-Alan Jones: Villeneuve and Jones were on-track rivals during the 1980 Formula 1 season. Both competed for the world championship, and their rivalry intensified in several races. Although they had moments of competitiveness and clashes on the track, they also held mutual respect for each other as talented drivers.

STIRLING MOSS

27

STIRLING MOSS.

He was a prominent British racing driver who competed in the 1950s and early 1960s.

-Formula 1 Career: He raced in Formula 1 from 1951 to 1961. During that time, he secured a total of 16 Grand Prix wins and finished second in the World Drivers' Championship in four consecutive years (1955, 1956, 1957, and 1958). Though he never clinched the championship, he is regarded as one of the greatest drivers in the history of Formula 1.

-Other Racing Disciplines: Beyond Formula 1, Moss participated in various motorsport disciplines, including endurance racing, rallying, and touring car races. He won numerous races and championships in these categories, showcasing his versatility and talent as a driver.

-Notable Wins: He achieved significant victories in his career, like the 1955 Mille Miglia, a famed endurance race in Italy, where he set a time record that remains unbeaten. He also triumphed in the British Grand Prix three times (1955, 1957, and 1959) and the Monaco Grand Prix three times (1956, 1960, and 1961).

-Personality and Legacy: He was renowned for his charisma, aggressive driving style, and his ability to push racing cars to their limits. He's also credited with helping advance safety in motorsport following a severe accident in 1962, which forced him to retire from professional racing. Throughout his life, Moss was recognized as one of the great ambassadors of British motorsport and a revered figure in the racing world.

Accidents:

-Spa-Francorchamps Grand Prix, 1960: During a qualifying lap for the Belgian Grand Prix, Moss lost control of his car at a high-speed corner and crashed into a bank. The accident resulted in severe injuries for Moss, who sustained a leg fracture and chest injuries.

-Goodwood, 1962: He suffered a severe accident while racing in an endurance event at the Goodwood circuit. His car left the track and hit an earth bank, resulting in serious injuries, including a concussion and a leg fracture. This accident marked the end of his professional career, as he chose to retire from racing.

Rivalries:

-Juan Manuel Fangio: Moss had an intense on-track rivalry with the legendary Argentine driver Juan Manuel Fangio. Both raced in the same era and had numerous duels on the circuits. Moss regarded Fangio as his primary rival and was determined to beat him. Although Moss never won a Formula 1 world championship, he is often remembered as one of the finest drivers to compete against Fangio.

-Mike Hawthorn: Moss also had a competitive rivalry with his fellow Briton, Mike Hawthorn. Both drivers were part of the legendary "gentleman racers" era of Formula 1 in the 1950s. They had numerous on-track duels, especially in the 1958 World Championship, in which Hawthorn clinched the title by only a single point over Moss.

EMERSON FITTIPALDI

28

EMERSON FITTIPALDI.

He is a former Brazilian racing driver born on December 12, 1946, in São Paulo, Brazil.

-Formula 1 Championships: He raced in Formula 1 during the 1970s. He won the world championship twice: in 1972 with Team Lotus and in 1974 with McLaren. In that latter year, he became the youngest driver to win a Formula 1 world championship at the time, at 27 years old.

-Team Lotus: He began his Formula 1 career with Team Lotus in 1970. During his tenure with Lotus, he achieved numerous victories and standout performances. He played a crucial role in the development of Lotus' single-seaters, and his smooth and precise driving style earned him recognition.

-McLaren: After his successful stint with Lotus, Fittipaldi joined Team McLaren in 1974. He continued achieving strong results and ultimately won the world championship that same year. His association with McLaren lasted until 1976.

-Participation in other categories: Apart from his Formula 1 career, Fittipaldi ventured into other racing categories. He raced in the CART IndyCar series in the United States, where he achieved significant successes. He won the series championship in 1989 and also claimed victory in the Indianapolis 500 in 1989 and 1993.

-Legacy and accolades: He is widely regarded as one of the most talented and successful drivers in Brazilian motorsport history. His success in Formula 1 and the CART IndyCar series has given him iconic status in the sport. In recognition of his achievements, he was inducted into the International Motorsports Hall of Fame and the Brazilian Motorsport Hall of Fame.

Accidents:

-Belgian Grand Prix 1970: In his first season in Formula 1 with Team Lotus, Fittipaldi suffered a severe crash on the opening lap of the race. He collided with the guardrail, and his single-seater was destroyed. Fortunately, Fittipaldi emerged unscathed.

-**British Grand Prix 1973:** During the race, Fittipaldi became involved in an incident with Jody Scheckter on the first lap. The crash caused damage to both single-seaters, forcing Fittipaldi to retire from the race.

-**South African Grand Prix 1976:** Fittipaldi experienced a severe accident during the practice session prior to the race. His single-seater lost a wheel and violently crashed into the barriers. The accident caused leg injuries, but he recovered and returned to racing later on.

Rivalries:

Throughout his motorsport career, Emerson Fittipaldi didn't have notable rivalries or significant conflicts with other drivers.

While he competed against several prominent drivers of his time, such as Jackie Stewart, Niki Lauda, and James Hunt, there were no intense or lasting rivalries recorded.

Fittipaldi was known to be a respectful and professional driver, and he maintained good relationships with his track colleagues.

Throughout his career, he earned the respect and admiration of many of his peers for his driving skill and his serious approach to competition.

CARLOS SAINZ

29

CARLOS SAINZ.

Whose full name is Carlos Sainz Vázquez de Castro, is a Spanish racing driver born on September 1, 1994, in Madrid, Spain.

-Early racing career: He began his career in karting at a young age and quickly showcased his talent. In 2009, he became the champion of the Spanish Formula Renault 2.0 and, the following year, won the European Formula Renault 2.0 championship.

-GP3 Series and Formula Renault 3.5: In 2012, Sainz competed in the GP3 Series, where he clinched the championship title with the MW Arden team. He then moved on to race in Formula Renault 3.5, where he won the championship in 2014 with the DAMS team.

-Formula 1: He made his Formula 1 debut in 2015 with the Toro Rosso team. During his time with Toro Rosso and later with Renault, he demonstrated his skill and consistency as a driver. In 2019, he joined the McLaren team, where he performed exceptionally well and established himself as one of the most talented drivers on the grid.

-Podiums and results: Throughout his Formula 1 career, Carlos Sainz has achieved several podiums and notable results. In total, he has secured more than 10 podiums and has finished in the top five on multiple occasions.

-Move to Ferrari: In 2021, Carlos Sainz joined the Ferrari team as a principal driver, marking a significant milestone in his career. He became teammates with Monegasque driver Charles Leclerc.

-Driving skills and style: He is known for his ability to quickly adapt to various track challenges and his capacity to extract the maximum performance from his car. He is a consistent, technical, and aggressive driver when necessary.

Accidents:

-Russian GP 2016: During the first lap of the race, Sainz had an accident in turn 2 with McLaren's driver, Jenson Button. The collision resulted in significant damages to Sainz's car and led to his withdrawal from the race.

-Canadian GP 2017: In the first qualifying session, Sainz lost control of his Toro Rosso at turn 3 and collided with the wall. The crash severely damaged his car, preventing him from participating in the rest of the qualifying session.

-British GP 2017: During the formation lap before the race, Sainz experienced an issue with his gearbox, leading to a crash and damages to his car. This forced Sainz to retire before the start of the race.

Rivalries:

-Max Verstappen: During their time together as teammates at Toro Rosso in 2015, Sainz and Verstappen had a competitive rivalry. Both drivers were young talents and were striving to make a mark. Their relationship became strained at times, especially after certain on-track incidents. However, since then, they have settled their rivalry and maintain mutual respect.

-Nico Hülkenberg: Sainz and Hülkenberg were teammates at Renault in 2018. While there wasn't an overt rivalry between them, they competed on equal terms and had a few brushes on the track, particularly in battles for position. Nonetheless, they also acknowledged each other for their driving abilities.

ESTEBAN OCON

30

ESTEBAN OCON.

He is a French racing driver.

-Early Career in Motorsport: Born on September 17, 1996, in Évreux, France, he started his career in karting and then progressed to single-seater categories. In 2014, he joined the Lotus young driver program (later renamed Renault).

-GP3 Series: In 2015, Ocon competed in the GP3 Series and clinched the championship with the ART Grand Prix team, securing five victories throughout the season.

-European Formula 3 Champion: In 2016, Ocon joined the Prema Powerteam in the European Formula 3 and emerged as the champion. Throughout that season, he achieved nine victories and 17 podium finishes.

-Formula 1 Debut: In 2016, Ocon made his Formula 1 debut with the Manor Racing team. He later competed for Force India (now Aston Martin) in 2017 and 2018. From 2019 onwards, he joined the Renault team (now known as Alpine F1 Team).

-Performance in Formula 1: Throughout his Formula 1 career, Esteban Ocon has proven to be a solid and talented driver. He has achieved notable results, including podium finishes and consistently scored points over several seasons.

Accidents:

-2018 Belgian Grand Prix: During the first lap of the race, Ocon and his teammate Sergio Pérez made contact exiting the Eau Rouge corner, resulting in a crash that led to both drivers retiring from the race.

-**2018 Singapore Grand Prix:** Ocon encountered an accident on lap 1 of the race when he collided with Kimi Räikkönen's car. The impact severely damaged his car, forcing him to retire from the race.

-**2019 Bahrain Grand Prix:** During the race, Ocon was involved in an incident with Renault's driver, Nico Hülkenberg. Both drivers made contact, resulting in damage to Ocon's car, which led to his retirement.

-**2020 Russian Grand Prix:** In the first lap of the race, Ocon was caught up in a multiple-car crash at turn 2. Several cars made contact, causing significant damage to Ocon's car and leading to his withdrawal from the race.

Rivalries:

He hasn't had any particularly intense or prolonged rivalry with another driver.

Generally, Ocon has focused on his performance and collaborated with his teammates to achieve positive results.

JACKIE ICKX

31

JACKIE ICKX.

His full name is Jacques Bernard "Jacky" Ickx, and he is a former Belgian racing driver born on January 1, 1945, in Brussels, Belgium.

Ickx had a distinguished career across various motorsport categories, including Formula 1, endurance racing, and rallies.

–Formula 1: He competed in Formula 1 from 1967 to 1979, representing several teams, including Ferrari, Lotus, Brabham, and McLaren. He achieved a total of 8 Grand Prix victories and secured 25 podium finishes in his career. He also finished runner-up in the world championship on two occasions, in 1969 and 1970.

–Endurance Racing: He is especially renowned for his successes in endurance races, including the 24 Hours of Le Mans. He won the 24 Hours of Le Mans six times, in 1969, 1975, 1976, 1977, 1981, and 1982. His ability to drive under challenging conditions and his strategic approach earned him the nickname "Rain Master."

–Dakar Rally: He competed in the Dakar Rally several times, with his best result being a third-place finish in 1983.

–Other Competitions: Beyond Formula 1, endurance races, and rallies, Ickx also took part in other motorsport competitions, like the World Sportscar Championship and the World Rallycross Championship.
Ickx is admired for his skill and versatility as a driver, as well as his strategic mindset and ability to handle various racing conditions.
His talent and success across different motorsport disciplines have granted him a prominent place in the sport's history.
After retiring from racing, Ickx has remained involved in motorsport, serving as an ambassador and consultant for various brands and motorsport-related events.

Accidents:

-1969 Belgian Grand Prix: During the Formula 1 race at the Spa-Francorchamps circuit, Ickx was involved in a severe accident on the first lap. His Ferrari car collided with Jackie Oliver's McLaren, causing Ickx's vehicle to flip and subsequently catch fire. Fortunately, Ickx was able to escape from the accident unharmed.

-1970 24 Hours of Le Mans: He was involved in an incident during the famed 1970 edition of the 24 Hours of Le Mans. While driving the Porsche 917 for the John Wyer Automotive Engineering team, Ickx had an accident when the car flipped after losing control in a corner. Despite the severity of the crash, Ickx and his co-driver, Peter Schetty, managed to exit the vehicle without serious injuries.

Rivalries:

Though no specific rivalries stand out, Ickx had thrilling on-track duels with other notable drivers of his era, such as Jackie Stewart, Jochen Rindt, Emerson Fittipaldi, and others.

These drivers competed in a highly competitive environment and continuously challenged each other in pursuit of race victories.

It's essential to note that, beyond on-track rivalries, Jackie Ickx was respected for his skill and his smooth and precise driving style.

He was recognized as an intelligent and strategic driver, capable of achieving strong results under different conditions and on various types of tracks.

Overall, Ickx was admired and respected by his fellow drivers and motorsport fans for his talent and dedication to the sport.

JODY
SCHECKTER

32

JODY SCHECKTER.

He is a former South African racing driver born on January 29, 1950, in East London, South Africa.

He is renowned for his successful Formula 1 career and for clinching the world championship in 1979.

-Formula 1 Career: He competed in Formula 1 during the 1970s and early 1980s. He made his debut in 1972 with the McLaren team and later went on to race for teams such as Tyrrell, Wolf, and Ferrari. He secured a total of 10 Grand Prix victories throughout his career.

-World Championship: The pinnacle of Scheckter's career came in 1979 when he won the Formula 1 World Championship with the Ferrari team. He became the first and, to date, the only South African driver to achieve this title. During that season, Scheckter displayed great consistency and clinched six wins in total.

-Driving Style: He was known for his methodical and calculated approach on the track. He was a careful and technical driver, which allowed him to maintain a steady pace and avoid costly errors. His strategic race approach was one of the keys to his success.

-Retirement: After his victory in the 1979 World Championship, Scheckter continued to race in Formula 1 until 1980. However, he chose to retire at the end of that season at the age of 30, citing his desire to spend more time with his family and step away from the inherent risks of the sport.

-Post-Racing Life: Since his retirement, Scheckter has remained active in the motorsport world. He has participated in exhibition races and has been involved in the development of high-performance cars. Additionally, he has established an organic farm in South Africa and has dedicated himself to regenerative farming.

Accidents:

He did not have any notable or severe accidents. Jody Scheckter was known for his ability to avoid risky situations and stay out of trouble on the track.

Rivalries:

During his Formula 1 career, Jody Scheckter did not have any particularly standout or lasting rivalries with other drivers.

However, it's common in the world of motorsport for temporary rivalries to arise based on on-track competition.

Throughout his career, Scheckter raced against several talented and experienced drivers, such as Niki Lauda, James Hunt, Mario Andretti, and Gilles Villeneuve, among others.

While he may have had moments of on-track rivalry with some of them, there are no emblematic rivalries that defined his trajectory in Formula 1.

Scheckter primarily focused on his own performance and competing at a high level without dwelling on lasting personal rivalries.

JACQUES
VILLENEUVE

33

JACQUES VILLENEUVE.

He is a Canadian racing driver born on April 9, 1971, in Saint-Jean-sur-Richelieu, Quebec.

He is known for his successful career in Formula 1 and his world championship title in 1997.

-Formula 1 Career: He made his debut in Formula 1 in 1996 with the Williams-Renault team. In his first year, he put on a remarkable performance, winning four races and finishing second in the championship, behind Damon Hill. However, in 1997, Villeneuve clinched the world championship title with seven wins, overcoming Michael Schumacher in the final race of the season.

-Driving Style and Personality: He was known for his aggressive and daring driving style. He wasn't afraid to challenge other drivers in overtaking maneuvers and often engaged in thrilling battles on the track. Off the track, Villeneuve was recognized for his outgoing personality and candidness when expressing his opinions.

-Career after Formula 1: After his stint in Formula 1, Villeneuve raced in other motorsport categories, including the IndyCar Series and the World Endurance Championship (WEC). In IndyCar, he achieved notable victories, including the prestigious Indianapolis 500 race in 1995. He also ventured into other disciplines, such as NASCAR races and rallycross.

-Legacy and Recognitions: He left a significant mark on Formula 1, especially by becoming the first and, to date, the only Canadian driver to win the world championship. His driving style and charisma made him a fan-favorite. In recognition of his achievements, he was inducted into the FIA Hall of Fame and was awarded the FIA Gold Trophy for Personality of the Year in 1997.

Accidents:

1996 Belgian Grand Prix: In his rookie Formula 1 season, Villeneuve suffered a major crash during qualifying at Spa-Francorchamps.

He lost control of his car and violently hit a tire barrier. Thankfully, he emerged unscathed.

-**1999 German Grand Prix:** During the race at the Hockenheim circuit, Villeneuve was involved in an incident with Ralf Schumacher. Both drivers collided at the Ostkurve turn, resulting in both of them retiring from the race.

-**2001 Canadian Grand Prix:** In his home race in Montreal, Villeneuve had an accident at the circuit's final turn. He crashed into the protective wall, damaging his car and forcing him to retire from the race.

-**2003 Brazilian Grand Prix:** He had an accident during the race in Interlagos. He lost control of his car at the Junção turn and crashed into the protective barriers, ending his race.

-**2005 German Grand Prix:** In qualifying at the Nürburgring, Villeneuve had a crash at turn 8. His car slid on the wet grass and collided with the tire barriers, resulting in significant damage to his car.

Rivalries:

-**Damon Hill:** The rivalry between Jacques Villeneuve and Damon Hill was one of the most intense in the 1990s. Both drivers raced for Williams and battled for the world championship in 1996. Villeneuve eventually clinched the championship that year, but his relationship with Hill became strained due to on-track incidents and disagreements off the track.

-Michael Schumacher: Villeneuve and Schumacher had several on-track clashes, with the most famous being the incident in the final race of the 1997 season in Jerez. Villeneuve tried to overtake Schumacher at the Dry Sac corner, and Schumacher, in an attempt to avoid being passed, deliberately crashed into Villeneuve's car. This incident resulted in Schumacher being disqualified from the race and allowed Villeneuve to secure the championship.

-Eddie Irvine: Villeneuve also had a rivalry with Eddie Irvine during his time at the BAR team in the 2000 season. The two drivers disagreed on several occasions, including an incident in the Brazilian Grand Prix where they touched, and both were affected.

HEIKKI KOVALAINEN

34

HEIKKI KOVALAINEN.

He is a Finnish racing driver.

-Birth and Formula 1 debut: Born on October 19, 1981, in Suomussalmi, Finland. He made his Formula 1 debut in 2007 with the Renault team.

-Formula 1 Career: He raced in Formula 1 for several years, driving for teams such as Renault, McLaren, and Lotus. His best season was in 2008 when he drove for McLaren and secured his first and only victory at the Hungarian Grand Prix. He also achieved several podiums throughout his career.

-GP2 Championship: Before moving to Formula 1, Kovalainen had success in the GP2 support category. He won the GP2 championship in 2005, showcasing his skill and talent as a driver.

-Participation in other categories: After leaving Formula 1, Kovalainen has raced in various motorsport categories. He has taken part in championships like the Superleague Formula, the FIA World Endurance Championship, and Japanese Super GT.

-Retirement from full-time racing: Although Kovalainen hasn't officially announced his retirement from motorsport, he has been away from full-time competition since 2017. However, he has participated in special events and high-performance car tests.

Accidents:

-2008 German Grand Prix: He suffered an accident during qualifying in Hockenheim. His car went off the track and crashed into the safety barriers. Fortunately, Kovalainen was unharmed in the incident.

-2009 Australian Grand Prix: During the race in Melbourne, Kovalainen was involved in a collision with Spanish driver Fernando Alonso. Both cars sustained damage, but again Kovalainen was not injured.

-2010 Belgian Grand Prix: In a rainy race at Spa-Francorchamps, Kovalainen had an accident on the first lap after contact with Italian driver Vitantonio Liuzzi. His car was damaged, and he had to retire from the race.

-2011 German Grand Prix: At Nürburgring, Kovalainen had a collision with German driver Adrian Sutil. His car was damaged, and he had to withdraw from the race.

Rivalries:

-Lewis Hamilton: Heikki Kovalainen was teammates with Lewis Hamilton at McLaren during the 2008 and 2009 seasons. Although there wasn't an overt rivalry between them, there was intense internal competition to prove their worth and performance in comparison to their teammate, especially given that Hamilton was considered one of the standout drivers of the time.

-Felipe Massa: During the 2008 season, Kovalainen was involved in an incident with Felipe Massa at the Canadian Grand Prix. Massa collided with the rear of Kovalainen's car, causing the latter to run off the track and lose positions. While there wasn't an ongoing rivalry after that incident, the collision created some tension between both drivers at the time.

FELIPE MASSA

35

FELIPE MASSA.

He is a Brazilian racing driver who competed in Formula 1 for several seasons.

-Formula 1 Career: He made his Formula 1 debut in 2002 with the Sauber team. He then joined Ferrari in 2006, where he spent the majority of his career. After his stint with Ferrari, he raced for the Williams team until his retirement from Formula 1 at the end of the 2017 season.

-World Runner-up: In 2008, Felipe Massa had a standout season in which he contended for the world championship. At the Brazilian Grand Prix that year, he secured a thrilling home victory but lost the championship by a single point to Lewis Hamilton. Despite not clinching the title, his performance that season earned him recognition and respect in Formula 1.

-Career at Ferrari: During his time at Ferrari, Felipe Massa was considered one of the team's lead drivers and achieved several successes. He won 11 races with the Italian team and secured a total of 36 podiums. He was teammates with Michael Schumacher, Kimi Räikkönen, and Fernando Alonso at different stages of his career.

-Formula 1 Retirement: He announced his retirement from Formula 1 at the end of the 2016 season, but briefly returned in 2017 to race for the Williams team. After his definitive retirement, he joined Formula E, where he competed for several seasons.

Accidents:

-2009 Hungarian Grand Prix: During the qualifying session for the 2009 Hungarian Grand Prix, Massa suffered a severe accident when a piece from Rubens Barrichello's car struck his helmet. As a result, Massa sustained head injuries and was out of competition for the remainder of the season. However, he fully recovered and returned to Formula 1 the following year.

-2002 Belgian Grand Prix: He had an accident on the first lap of the race when he collided with Pedro de la Rosa. Both drivers retired from the race.

-2003 German Grand Prix: He had a collision with Mark Webber on the first lap, resulting in both drivers retiring.

-2004 Australian Grand Prix: Massa collided with Gianmaria Bruni on the first lap, causing both drivers to retire.

-2008 European Grand Prix: He had an accident when exiting the pits, losing control of his car and crashing into the barriers. Fortunately, he did not sustain serious injuries.

-2011 Singapore Grand Prix: Massa collided with Vitantonio Liuzzi on the first lap of the race, leading to both drivers retiring.

Rivalries:

-Rivalry with Lewis Hamilton: The rivalry between Massa and Hamilton peaked in the 2008 season. Both drivers vied for the world championship, and their relationship became tense after several on-track incidents. The most notable was during the Singapore Grand Prix, where Massa accused Hamilton of dirty play and causing his accident.

-Rivalry with Fernando Alonso: Massa and Alonso were teammates at Ferrari from 2010 to 2013. While they had moments of collaboration, there was also internal rivalry and tensions. The rivalry reached its peak during the 2010 German Grand Prix when Massa was ordered by the team to let Alonso pass, generating controversy and discontent within the team.

-Rivalry with Romain Grosjean: Massa and Grosjean had several on-track confrontations during the 2012 season. There were incidents at the Belgian Grand Prix and the Japanese Grand Prix where both drivers were involved in collisions and criticized each other's driving styles.

-Rivalry with Sergio Pérez: Massa and Pérez had a few run-ins on the track during the 2013 season. The most notable was during the Canadian Grand Prix, where they had a crash that led to both drivers retiring from the race. Massa voiced his frustration with Pérez and accused him of driving aggressively.

PASTOR
MALDONADO

36

PASTOR MALDONADO.

He is a Venezuelan racing driver born on March 9, 1985, in Maracay, Venezuela.

Maldonado began his career in karting and then moved up to the single-seater categories in Europe.

In 2007, he became a test driver for the Williams Formula 1 team.

In 2011, he secured his first Formula 1 podium by finishing third at the Spanish Grand Prix.

The highlight of Maldonado's career came at the 2012 Spanish Grand Prix, where he achieved a surprising victory from pole position.

It was the first win for a Venezuelan driver in Formula 1 and also the first victory for the Williams team in several years.

However, there was significant controversy, as a dispute emerged on the race's final lap when Maldonado and Alonso engaged in a fierce battle for the lead.

At turn 3, Maldonado made a defensive move, and Alonso tried to overtake him on the outside.

However, both drivers touched, and Alonso ended up off the track, allowing Maldonado to maintain the lead and cross the finish line in first place.

This incident sparked a debate about whether the contact between Maldonado and Alonso was a racing incident or if Maldonado had been overly aggressive in his defense.

Some critics argued that Maldonado should have left more space to avoid contact, while others defended his right to protect his position.

Furthermore, Maldonado's career was also marked by numerous incidents and controversies.

-On-track incidents: Maldonado was known for his aggressive driving style, leading him to be involved in numerous collisions and track incidents. He was penalized several times for risky maneuvers and for causing accidents that affected other drivers.

-Collision with Lewis Hamilton: At the 2011 European Grand Prix, Maldonado and Lewis Hamilton had an incident on the race's final lap. Both drivers touched and ended up off the track, resulting in both retiring from the race. This collision drew criticism towards Maldonado and became one of the most controversial moments of his career.

-Penalties for infractions: Throughout his Formula 1 career, Maldonado received various penalties for on-track infractions. These included penalties for illegal overtakes, clashes with other drivers, and unsporting conduct.

-Controversial comments: Maldonado also stirred controversy with some of his remarks in the media. On some occasions, his statements were deemed controversial or inappropriate, sparking criticism and controversy in the motorsport world.

After his stint at Williams, Maldonado competed for the Lotus Formula 1 team in 2014 and 2015, but he didn't achieve similar standout results.

In 2016, his final season in Formula 1, he raced for the Renault team.

Since leaving Formula 1, Maldonado has competed in other motorsport categories, such as the World Endurance Championship (WEC) and Formula E.

Accidents:

-2011 Monaco Grand Prix: During the third qualifying session, Maldonado lost control of his Williams exiting the Sainte Devote corner and hit the barriers.

The crash resulted in significant damage to his car and forced him to start the race from the last position.

-2012 Belgian Grand Prix: On the first lap of the race, Maldonado made contact with McLaren driver, Lewis Hamilton, at the Les Combes corner, causing Hamilton to retire from the race. Maldonado also sustained damage to his car and had to retire later due to the damage from the incident.

-2014 Belgian Grand Prix: During qualifying, Maldonado lost control of his Lotus at the Blanchimont corner and crashed violently into the barriers. Fortunately, he emerged unscathed from the crash, but his car suffered significant damage.

-2015 Austrian Grand Prix: During the race, Maldonado collided with Felipe Nasr's Sauber at turn 2, causing both drivers to retire from the race. The incident was investigated by the stewards, and Maldonado received a five-place grid penalty for the following race.

Rivalries:

-Sergio Pérez: Maldonado and Mexican driver Sergio Pérez had several on-track clashes. At the 2012 Monaco Grand Prix, Maldonado and Pérez made contact at the tunnel corner, resulting in both drivers retiring. There were also incidents in other races that added tension between them.

-Lewis Hamilton: Maldonado and British World Champion Lewis Hamilton had some tense moments on the track. At the 2011 Belgian Grand Prix, Maldonado made a controversial move and collided with Hamilton, leading to Hamilton's retirement from the race. They also clashed on other occasions, heightening the rivalry between the two drivers.

-Esteban Gutiérrez: Another notable rivalry of Maldonado was with Mexican driver Esteban Gutiérrez. At the 2014 Bahrain Grand Prix, Maldonado made an aggressive move and collided with Gutiérrez, flipping his Sauber. This incident drew criticism towards Maldonado and fueled the rivalry between both drivers.

ROBERT KUBICA

37

ROBERT KUBICA.

He is a Polish racing driver born on December 7, 1984, in Krakow, Poland.

He began his career in karting and then progressed to single-seater categories.

-Formula 1 Career: Kubica made his Formula 1 debut in 2006 with the BMW Sauber team. During his F1 career, Kubica was known for his speed and skill on the track. His greatest success came at the 2008 Canadian Grand Prix, where he achieved his first and only Formula 1 victory. Additionally, he secured a total of 12 podium finishes and one pole position throughout his career.

-Return to Racing: After his accident in 2011, Kubica spent several years recovering and working diligently to return to racing. He made his competition comeback in 2017, participating in various championships and tests in sports cars and rallies.

-Participation in Other Categories: Besides his involvement in Formula 1, Kubica has also competed in other motorsport categories. He has raced in championships such as the World Rally Championship (WRC) and the DTM (Deutsche Tourenwagen Masters), where he has demonstrated strong performance and achieved good results on some occasions.

-Return to Formula 1: In 2019, Kubica managed to return to Formula 1 as a primary driver with the Williams team. Although the team was facing performance challenges, Kubica showcased his determination and skills on the track. However, by the end of the season, his contract with Williams was not renewed.

Robert Kubica is admired for his natural talent and aggressive driving style.

Accidents:

Accident at the Rally di Andora (2011): Kubica went off the road and crashed into a guardrail during the rally. He suffered a fracture in his right arm, injuries to his right hand, and a partial amputation of the forearm. This accident had a significant impact on his career and kept him out of Formula 1 for several seasons.

Accident at the Canadian Grand Prix (2007): During the Formula 1 race at the Montreal circuit, Kubica had a spectacular crash at turn 10. He hit the side barrier and was then struck by another car. Fortunately, Kubica only suffered a mild concussion and a sprained ankle.

Accident at the Belgian Grand Prix (2007): At the famous Eau Rouge corner on the Spa-Francorchamps circuit, Kubica had a massive crash after losing control of his car due to wet conditions. The car smashed into the tire barriers, but Kubica managed to walk away unharmed.

Another accident at the Canadian Grand Prix (2007): During the free practice sessions for the Montreal race, Kubica had another crash. He lost control of his car and hit the containment barriers violently. He was taken to the hospital for checks, but fortunately, he did not suffer serious injuries.

Rivalries:

-Rivalry with Sebastian Vettel: In the 2010 Formula 1 season, Kubica and Vettel had several on-track encounters that led to a rivalry. At the Japanese Grand Prix, Kubica and Vettel touched while competing for position, resulting in damage to Kubica's front wing and a penalty for Vettel. Later, at the Turkish Grand Prix, Kubica and Vettel collided again, this time forcing Kubica to retire. These incidents heightened the tension between the two drivers.

-Rivalry with Felipe Massa: In the 2010 Formula 1 season, Kubica and Massa also had several on-track encounters that led to some rivalry. At the Japanese Grand Prix, Kubica and Massa made contact on the first lap, resulting in damage to Kubica's front wing and a puncture in Massa's tire. At the Singapore Grand Prix, Kubica tried to overtake Massa, but they ended up colliding and Kubica had to retire from the race.

-Rivalry with Adrian Sutil: Kubica and Sutil had several clashes on track during the 2010 Formula 1 season. At the Australian Grand Prix, Kubica and Sutil made contact during an overtaking maneuver, which caused Sutil to retire from the race. At the Japanese Grand Prix, Kubica and Sutil had another on-track incident, leading Sutil to label Kubica as a "dangerous" driver after the race.

DAVID
COULTHARD

38

DAVID COULTHARD.

He is a former British racing driver who competed in Formula 1 for 15 seasons, from 1994 to 2008. He was born on March 27, 1971, in Twynholm, Scotland.

-Formula 1 Career: He made his Formula 1 debut in 1994 with the Williams team, where he was a teammate of Ayrton Senna until the tragic death of the Brazilian. Subsequently, Coulthard moved to race for the McLaren team, where he spent the majority of his Formula 1 career. He also had a brief stint with Red Bull Racing in the final years of his career.

-Wins and Podiums: Throughout his Formula 1 career, Coulthard secured a total of 13 wins and 62 podium finishes. His victories include the Monaco Grand Prix, the British Grand Prix, and the Australian Grand Prix, among others.

-Career in Top-tier Teams: He had the opportunity to race for top-tier teams during his career, such as Williams and McLaren. During his time at McLaren, he was teammates with legendary Finnish driver Mika Häkkinen, and together they formed one of the most successful and respected driver pairings in Formula 1 history.

-Personality and Leadership: He was known for his charisma and his ability to communicate both on and off the track. He was seen as a leader in the paddock and was respected for his work ethic and professionalism.

-Retirement and Subsequent Career: After retiring from Formula 1 in 2008, Coulthard remained involved in motorsports. He worked as a race commentator and analyst for the BBC and later for Channel 4 in the UK. He also participated in endurance racing competitions, including the famed 24 Hours of Le Mans.

Accidents:

-Australian Grand Prix 1995: On the first lap of the race, Coulthard was involved in a chain-reaction accident that forced him out of the competition. Multiple cars collided in turn 3, and Coulthard suffered damage to his single-seater and had to retire.

-**Brazilian Grand Prix 2001:** In a race held under intense rain conditions, Coulthard lost control of his car in turn 3 and crashed into the wall. The accident prematurely ended his race and resulted in significant damage to his vehicle.

-**German Grand Prix 2003:** During the qualifying session, Coulthard had an accident at turn 13 of the Hockenheim circuit. His car smashed into the wall, causing considerable damage to the vehicle and forcing him to start the race from the back of the grid.

-**Monaco Grand Prix 2006:** Coulthard had a crash during the free practice session at the swimming pool turn. He lost control of his car and hit the safety barriers, severely damaging his vehicle and ruling him out of the race qualification.

Rivalries:

-**Rivalry with Mika Häkkinen:** He was Mika Häkkinen's teammate at McLaren for several seasons. While they had a good relationship off the track, on the track rivalries and tensions arose as both drivers competed for the team's lead and championships. This internal rivalry led to tense moments and clashes between them in some races.

-**Rivalry with Michael Schumacher:** He faced off against Michael Schumacher, one of Formula 1's most successful drivers, on several occasions. While they didn't have an intense rivalry in terms of on-track incidents, there was competition and moments of contention between them during races.

-**Rivalry with Jarno Trulli:** Coulthard and Jarno Trulli had several on-track disputes and altercations. At the 2000 German Grand Prix, Coulthard and Trulli were involved in a first-lap incident, leading to both drivers retiring from the race. This situation created tension between them, and they continued to have competitive encounters in subsequent races.

NICO
HÜLKENBERG

39

NICO HÜLKENBERG.

Nicolas Hülkenberg is a German racing driver.

He was born on August 19, 1987, in Emmerich am Rhein, Germany.

Throughout his career, Hülkenberg has competed in various motor racing categories, but he is best known for his participation in Formula 1.

Hülkenberg made his Formula 1 debut in 2010 with the Williams team.

During his rookie season, he impressed by securing a pole position in his debut race at the Brazilian Grand Prix, becoming the first rookie to achieve this feat.

However, he was unable to maintain that position and finished in tenth place.

During his time at Williams, Hülkenberg displayed flashes of his driving talent and skills, but the team struggled and couldn't achieve consistent results.

In 2012, Hülkenberg joined the Force India team, where he had a notable season.

He achieved his best Formula 1 result up to that point by finishing fourth at the Belgian Grand Prix.

He continued racing with Force India in the following seasons and displayed solid and consistent performance, scoring points regularly and outperforming his teammate on multiple occasions.

In 2017, Hülkenberg joined the Renault team, where he spent three seasons.

During his time with Renault, he achieved some notable results, including a sixth-place finish at the 2019 German Grand Prix.

However, the team was not in a position to consistently compete for victories or podiums.

In addition to his participation in Formula 1, Hülkenberg has raced in other motor racing categories.

He has competed in the 24 Hours of Le Mans, where he achieved victory in the LMP1 category in 2015 with the Porsche team.

He has also raced in the IMSA WeatherTech SportsCar Championship series in the United States.

Despite his talent and driving skills, Hülkenberg has not had the opportunity to race for a top-tier Formula 1 team and has not managed to stand on the podium in the category.

Despite this, he is widely recognized for his speed and consistency and is considered one of the most talented drivers without a podium in Formula 1 history.

Accidents:

-Brazilian Grand Prix 2010: He had an accident on the last lap of the race while battling for position with Sebastian Vettel. He lost control of his car at the Ferradura turn and crashed into the barrier, resulting in his retirement from the race.

-Australian Grand Prix 2013: On the first lap of the race, Hülkenberg had a collision with Esteban Gutiérrez at turn 1. Hülkenberg's car flipped and rolled several times before coming to a stop. Fortunately, both drivers emerged unharmed.

-Belgian Grand Prix 2018: On the first lap of the race, Hülkenberg was involved in a chain collision that involved multiple drivers, including Fernando Alonso and Charles Leclerc. The incident resulted in the retirement from the race for Hülkenberg and other competitors.

-Abu Dhabi Grand Prix 2018: On the formation lap before the race, Hülkenberg made contact with Romain Grosjean, causing damage to his car. As a result, Hülkenberg had to retire from the race before it started.

Rivalries:

-Sergio Pérez: Hülkenberg and Pérez were teammates at Force India in the 2014, 2015, and 2016 seasons. While there was no intense rivalry between them, they had some on-track clashes due to battles for position. Both drivers proved to be competitive and often faced off in thrilling duels.

-Kevin Magnussen: Hülkenberg and Magnussen had several on-track confrontations during the 2017 season when both raced for different teams. There were instances where they made contact or had close battles while fighting for positions on the track.

EDDIE IRVINE

40

EDDIE IRVINE.

He is a former Formula 1 driver born on November 10, 1965, in Newtownards, Northern Ireland.

He competed in Formula 1 from 1993 to 2002 and is best known for his time as a Ferrari driver.

-Formula 1 Career: He made his Formula 1 debut in 1993 with the Jordan team. He later joined Ferrari in 1996, where he spent the next four seasons as Michael Schumacher's teammate.

-Success with Ferrari: During his time at Ferrari, Irvine achieved his most significant successes in Formula 1. In the 1999 season, he claimed four victories and finished second in the Drivers' Championship, behind his teammate Schumacher. It was a standout season for him as he came close to winning the world championship.

-Personality and Controversies: He is known for being a driver with an outgoing and candid personality. He often spoke straightforwardly and was not afraid to voice his opinions. This sometimes led to controversies and confrontations with other drivers and paddock members.

-Retirement and Later Life: After leaving Formula 1 at the end of the 2002 season, Eddie Irvine retired from high-level car racing. However, he remained active in the motorsport world and has participated in endurance races, such as the 24 Hours of Le Mans.

Accidents:

-Argentina Grand Prix 1997: In this incident, Irvine had an accident during the warm-up lap before the race. He lost control of his car and crashed into the safety barriers at turn 8 of the Buenos Aires circuit. The impact caused significant damage to the car, forcing him to retire from the race before it started.

-Australian Grand Prix 1999: During the first lap of this race, Irvine was involved in a multi-car accident at turn 3. Several collisions among multiple cars caused chaos on the track, and Irvine's car was damaged in the incident. Although he was able to continue in the race, he later had to retire due to damages to his car.

Rivalries:

-Michael Schumacher: Eddie Irvine's most well-known rivalry was with his Ferrari teammate, Michael Schumacher. Irvine joined the Ferrari team in 1996 as Schumacher's number two driver. During the seasons they were together at Ferrari, tensions and rivalries arose due to competitiveness and the battle for the world championship. In 1999, Irvine had the chance to compete for the world title after Schumacher suffered an injury, further intensifying the rivalry between the two drivers.

-Mika Hakkinen: Eddie Irvine also had a rivalry with Finnish driver Mika Hakkinen, who was Irvine's main competitor in the fight for the world championship in the 1999 season. Irvine and Hakkinen clashed in several races during that season, and their on-track battles were intense and thrilling. Although Irvine didn't manage to beat Hakkinen in the championship battle, their rivalry added excitement and competition to the sport.

GERHARD BERGER

41

GERHARD BERGER.

He is a racing driver born on August 27, 1959, in Austria.

He is known for his successful career in Formula 1, where he competed from 1984 to 1997.

Throughout his career, Berger took part in 210 Formula 1 Grands Prix, achieving 10 wins, 48 podiums, and 12 pole positions.

Berger began his Formula 1 career with the ATS team in 1984, but it was in 1986 when he joined the Benetton team, where he tasted his first success by winning his inaugural race at the Mexico Grand Prix.

After a brief stint with the Ferrari team in 1987, Berger returned to Benetton in 1988.

However, it was in 1989 when Berger achieved his greatest success in Formula 1, joining the McLaren team, where he formed a successful partnership with Ayrton Senna.

Together, they won several Grands Prix and helped McLaren secure the constructors' championship in 1988 and 1990.

After his time at McLaren, Berger returned to Ferrari in 1993, racing for them for five seasons.

During his time at Ferrari, Berger clinched several wins and became one of the team's mainstays.

In 1994, he experienced a tragic accident at the San Marino Grand Prix, resulting in the death of his teammate, Ayrton Senna, which deeply affected Berger and the Formula 1 world at large.

Berger retired from Formula 1 at the end of the 1997 season, but he remained involved in motorsports.

After his retirement, he became an advisor for BMW in their Formula 1 program and also held management positions in the Toro Rosso team.

Off the track, Berger is known for his friendly personality and sense of humor.

After his retirement, he has participated in various motorsport events and has been active in businesses related to the sport.

Accidents:

-San Marino Grand Prix 1989: In this incident, Berger suffered a severe accident during free practice. His car violently crashed into the barriers at the Tamburello corner of the Imola circuit. The accident was caused by a rear suspension failure on his Ferrari. Fortunately, Berger managed to exit the car on his own, but he suffered burns on his hands and was taken to the hospital for treatment.

-Australian Grand Prix 1991: During qualifying for this race, Berger had another shocking crash. At the Swan corner, his McLaren lost traction on an oil patch and crashed into the wall. The car sustained significant damage, but Berger walked away unscathed.

Rivalries:

-Ayrton Senna: Berger and Ayrton Senna had a rivalry on the track but also shared a close friendship off it. Both drivers were teammates at McLaren during the 1988 to 1992 seasons. The rivalry between them peaked in 1990 when they had several on-track incidents, including a crash at the Japan Grand Prix, resulting in both retiring. Despite these confrontations, Berger and Senna held mutual respect and collaborated for the success of the McLaren team.

-Alain Prost: Berger also had a rivalry with Alain Prost, one of the most successful drivers in Formula 1 history. They competed on different teams over several years, but their on-track encounters were often intense. The most notable rivalry between Berger and Prost occurred in the 1989 season when Prost was at McLaren and Berger at Ferrari. Their most prominent clash took place at the Portugal Grand Prix, where they had an on-track incident resulting in both drivers retiring.

RUBENS
BARRICHELLO

42

RUBENS BARRICHELLO.

He is a racing driver born on May 23, 1972, in Brazil.

He is recognized for his successful career in Formula 1, where he competed for 19 seasons, from 1993 to 2011.

Barrichello is one of the longest-serving drivers in Formula 1 history, having participated in a total of 326 Grand Prix races, making him one of the most experienced drivers of all time.

Barrichello began his Formula 1 career with the Jordan team in 1993 and then joined the Stewart team in 1997.

However, it was during his time with the Ferrari team where he achieved his most notable success.

From 2000 to 2005, Barrichello was teammate to the legendary driver Michael Schumacher at Ferrari.

During that period, he managed to secure a total of 9 wins and contributed to Ferrari's dominance in the constructors' championship.

After his stint with Ferrari, Barrichello raced for the Honda, Brawn GP, and Williams teams.

In 2009, while driving for Brawn GP, Barrichello achieved his highest accolade in Formula 1 by finishing second in the drivers' championship, just behind his teammate Jenson Button.

He also secured a total of 11 wins, 68 podiums, and 14 pole positions throughout his Formula 1 career.

In addition to his participation in Formula 1, Barrichello has competed in other motorsport categories, such as the IndyCar Series and Stock Car Brasil.

After his retirement from Formula 1 in 2011, Barrichello continued racing in other categories and became a television commentator and a public figure in his home country, Brazil.

Accidents:

-San Marino Grand Prix 1994: During the qualifying for this Grand Prix, Barrichello had a severe accident at the Variante Bassa turn of the Imola circuit. He lost control of his car and crashed into the wall at high speed. The impact was very strong, and Barrichello suffered a broken nose and a concussion. This accident happened at the same race where driver Ayrton Senna lost his life, leaving a significant mark on Barrichello and the Formula 1 community in general.

-German Grand Prix 2000: During the qualifying for this race at the Hockenheim circuit, Barrichello had a high-speed crash. While driving at over 300 km/h, his car went off the track and rolled several times before coming to a stop. Fortunately, Barrichello emerged unscathed from the crash, but the car suffered severe damage.

Rivalries:

-Michael Schumacher: Barrichello's most known rivalry was with his teammate at Ferrari, Michael Schumacher. During their time together at Ferrari (2000-2005), Schumacher was the team's lead driver and was given preference in various situations, leading to tensions between the two drivers. Barrichello was often required to yield positions or act as Schumacher's wingman for the benefit of the team. However, despite these tensions, Barrichello and Schumacher also maintained a relationship of respect and collaboration on the track.

-Jenson Button: Another notable rivalry for Barrichello was with British driver Jenson Button. Both were teammates at the Honda team (later renamed Brawn GP) during the 2006 to 2009 seasons. In 2009, Barrichello and Button competed for the world championship, with Button ultimately taking the title. During that season, tensions and rivalries arose between the two drivers as they battled for supremacy within the team.

JARNO TRULLI

43

JARNO TRULLI.

He is an Italian racing driver born on July 13, 1974, in Pescara, Italy.

He is known for his successful career in Formula 1, where he competed for 15 seasons, from 1997 to 2011.

Trulli began his career in karting before moving up to single-seater categories. He made his Formula 1 debut in 1997 with the Minardi team.

He then went on to race for teams such as Prost, Jordan, Renault, Toyota, and Lotus (later renamed as Caterham).

During his time in Formula 1, Trulli showcased notable skills in qualifying, being known for his fast pace in a flying lap.

One of the highlights of Trulli's career was his sole Formula 1 win at the 2004 Monaco Grand Prix.

He was driving for the Renault team at that time and managed to hold off Ferrari drivers, Michael Schumacher and Rubens Barrichello, to secure the victory in a chaotic race under wet conditions.

In addition to his Monaco win, Trulli achieved a total of 11 podiums in Formula 1 and secured four pole positions throughout his career.

He was known for his ability to defend his position on the track and for his solid and consistent driving style.

Trulli retired from Formula 1 at the end of the 2011 season.

After his retirement, he continued to participate in various racing competitions, including the World Endurance Championship (WEC) and the Italian Touring Car Championship.

Accidents:

-2004 Monaco Grand Prix: He had an accident at the famous Casino turn during qualifying. The incident severely damaged his race car, forcing him to start from the back of the grid in the race.

-2005 Canadian Grand Prix: During the race, Trulli collided with McLaren driver, Kimi Räikkönen, at the first corner. Both drivers had to retire due to the damage to their cars.

-2005 German Grand Prix: In this event, Trulli was involved in a multi-car crash on the first lap, resulting in several drivers retiring, including himself.

-2006 Brazilian Grand Prix: Trulli had a crash during free practice when his car destabilized on a fast corner and hit the safety barriers. Fortunately, he walked away unscathed, but he was unable to take part in the qualifying and the race.

Rivalries:

-Rivalry with Fernando Alonso: Trulli and Alonso were teammates at Renault during the 2003 and 2004 seasons. Their rivalry peaked at the 2004 Monaco Grand Prix when Trulli was made to give up his position to Alonso due to team orders. This caused friction between them and contributed to Trulli's departure from the team at the end of the season.

-Rivalry with Ralf Schumacher: Trulli and Ralf Schumacher clashed on several occasions throughout their respective careers. There were notable incidents, such as the 2003 French Grand Prix, where Trulli and Schumacher collided, resulting in both drivers retiring from the race.

-Rivalry with Giancarlo Fisichella: Trulli and Fisichella were teammates at Renault in the 2005 season. There was an intense rivalry between them as they competed directly for results on the track. This rivalry peaked at the 2005 Australian Grand Prix when both drivers collided while battling for position.

-Rivalry with Michael Schumacher: While it wasn't a constant rivalry, Trulli and Michael Schumacher had some notable confrontations. At the 2003 French Grand Prix, Trulli was leading the race and fiercely defended his position against Schumacher, who was trying to overtake him. This led to an intense on-track duel, and Schumacher eventually managed to get past him.

LANCE STROLL

44

LANCE STROLL.

He is a Canadian racing driver born on October 29, 1998, in Montreal, Canada.

-Early in Motorsport: Stroll began his career in karting, where he found success, winning multiple national and regional championships. Then, in 2014, he transitioned to single-seater categories.

-Formula 3 and European Formula 3 Championship: In 2015, Stroll raced in the European Formula 3 Championship with Prema Powerteam. He put up a stellar performance and clinched the championship with a total of 14 victories, setting several records along the way.

-Formula 1 Debut: In 2017, Stroll made his Formula 1 debut with the Williams team. His entrance into Formula 1 was partly backed by the financial support of his father, Lawrence Stroll, a billionaire businessman. In his rookie season, he secured his first podium at the Azerbaijan Grand Prix, becoming the youngest driver to achieve a podium in Formula 1.

-Racing Point / Aston Martin: In 2019, Stroll joined Racing Point (later renamed Aston Martin in 2021) after his father led a consortium of investors that acquired the team. As a driver for Racing Point / Aston Martin, Stroll has secured multiple points and has shown flashes of speed across various races.

-Driving Style and Strengths: Stroll is known for his ability to quickly adapt to different track conditions and his efficient tire management. He has proven to be strong in wet conditions and has achieved good results in chaotic races. Additionally, he is an aggressive driver in the opening laps of races.

Criticism and Controversies:

-Financial Backing: One of the main criticisms directed at Lance Stroll is that his arrival in Formula 1 was primarily due to his financial backing. His father, Lawrence Stroll, is a billionaire businessman and has been a significant financial supporter of his son's career. This has led to the perception that Lance secured his place in Formula 1 mainly due to his money and connections rather than his talent as a driver.

-Williams and Racing Point: In 2017, Lance Stroll made his Formula 1 debut with the Williams team. During his time at Williams, there were criticisms over whether he was ready to compete in Formula 1 at such a young age, as he was only 18 at the time. Moreover, some argued that his financial connection with his father helped secure his seat on the team.

In 2019, Lance Stroll joined the Racing Point team (now Aston Martin F1 Team). Controversy arose when the team was accused of illegally copying the brake design of Mercedes. Although the FIA fined the team, Stroll and his teammates faced no individual sanctions.

-On-track Performance: In addition to criticisms related to his financial backing, Lance Stroll has also faced divided opinions regarding his on-track performance. Some see him as a talented driver who has shown flashes of skill and speed. On various occasions, he has achieved impressive results, such as podium finishes at the 2017 Azerbaijan Grand Prix and the 2020 Italian Grand Prix.

However, others argue that Stroll has struggled to maintain consistent performance and has made costly errors during races. These criticisms have been heightened due to comparison with his teammate, leading to questions about his true level of talent in Formula 1.

Accidents:

-2017 Russian Grand Prix: During the race's opening lap, Stroll was involved in a chain-reaction crash at Turn 3.
His car suffered significant damage, and he had to retire from the race.

-2018 Canadian Grand Prix: On the race's opening lap, Stroll had an incident with Toro Rosso's Brendon Hartley. Both cars collided, and Stroll had to retire from the race due to damage to his car.

-2019 French Grand Prix: During the race, Stroll was involved in a crash with McLaren's Lando Norris at Turn 11. The incident resulted in damage to the cars, and Stroll had to retire from the race.

-2019 German Grand Prix: In a chaotic race with challenging track conditions due to rain, Stroll crashed at Turn 8 and had to retire from the race due to damage to his car.

-**2020 Belgian Grand Prix:** On the race's opening lap, Stroll had an incident with AlphaTauri's Pierre Gasly at Turn 9. The collision resulted in damage to the cars, and Stroll had to retire from the race.

Rivalries:

-**Rivalry with Felipe Massa:** In his debut Formula 1 season in 2017, Stroll was teammates with Felipe Massa at Williams. Although there wasn't a direct rivalry and they worked together as teammates, Stroll was consistently compared to Massa due to his status as a rookie backed by a wealthy father.

-**Rivalry with Esteban Ocon:** In the 2018 season, Stroll and Esteban Ocon were teammates at Force India (later renamed Racing Point). Throughout the season, tensions arose between them due to several on-track incidents, including a crash at the Azerbaijan Grand Prix. These tensions led to a deterioration in the relationship between the two drivers.

-**Rivalry with Sergio Pérez:** In 2019, Stroll became teammates with Sergio Pérez at Racing Point. This rivalry intensified due to both drivers vying for the team's number 1 driver status and on-track leadership. While both drivers have had their moments of success, there have also been some friction and collisions between them.

-**Rivalry with Sebastian Vettel:** In 2021, Stroll became teammates with Sebastian Vettel at Aston Martin. While there hasn't been open rivalry or significant conflicts between them, the presence of a four-time world champion like Vettel in the team has led to comparisons and indirect competition between the two drivers.

MICK
SCHUMACHER

45

MICK SCHUMACHER.

Michael Schumacher is a German racing driver born on March 22, 1999, in Vufflens-le-Château, Switzerland.

He is the son of the legendary seven-time Formula 1 World Champion, Michael Schumacher.

-Start in Motorsport: Mick Schumacher began his career in karting, just like many elite drivers. In 2015, he transitioned to single-seater categories and competed in the ADAC Formula 4.

-European Formula 3 Championship: In 2018, Schumacher raced in the European Formula 3 Championship with Prema Theodore Racing. During that season, he saw a notable improvement in performance and clinched the championship with a total of eight wins. His title in European Formula 3 caught the attention of many in the motorsport world.

-Rise to Formula 2: Following his success in European Formula 3, Schumacher moved up to Formula 2 in 2019, joining Prema Racing. In his initial seasons, he showed steady progress and gained experience in a category regarded as the gateway to Formula 1.

-Formula 1 Debut: In 2021, Schumacher made his much-anticipated Formula 1 debut with the Haas team. He became the second member of the Schumacher family to reach the pinnacle of motorsport. His Formula 1 entry was met with significant media attention due to his father's fame and legacy.

-Driving Style and Strengths: Mick Schumacher is known for his methodical approach and consistent improvement. He has displayed solid technical skills and good tire management. He has also been praised for his work ethic and dedication to learning and quickly adapting to the challenges of Formula 1.

-Comparisons with his father: Given his father's legacy, Mick Schumacher has faced constant comparisons with Michael Schumacher. While these comparisons are inevitable, Mick has expressed his desire to carve his own path and create his own legacy in motorsport.

Accidents:

-2019 Formula 2 Spanish Grand Prix: He was involved in a multi-car accident on the first lap of the Formula 2 race in Barcelona. The incident resulted in his car flipping over and his subsequent retirement from the race.

-2019 Formula 2 Qualifying in Austria: He had an accident during the qualifying session at the Red Bull Ring, damaging his car and affecting his starting grid position for the race.

-2019 Formula 2 Qualifying in Russia: During the qualifying session in Sochi, Schumacher had a crash at turn 4, which resulted in damage to his car and hampered his performance in the subsequent race.

Rivalries:

Mick Schumacher has not yet had any notable rivalries or significant conflicts with other drivers in his short career in Formula 1.

As a rookie driver, he is focused on adapting to the Formula 1 environment and developing his driving skills.

LANDO NORRIS

46

LANDO NORRIS.

He is a British racing driver born on November 13, 1999, in Bristol, England.

-Start in Motorsport: He began his career in karting, where he was highly successful and won numerous championships at both national and international levels. In 2015, he transitioned to single-seater categories.

-European Formula 3 Championship: In 2017, Norris competed in the European Formula 3 Championship and displayed an impressive performance. He won the championship with nine victories and was recognized as one of the most promising young talents in motorsport.

-McLaren and Formula 1: In 2018, Norris joined the McLaren team as a development and test driver. The following year, in 2019, he was promoted to McLaren's Formula 1 team as a full-time driver, becoming one of the youngest drivers to debut in the category.

-Seasons in Formula 1: Since his debut in Formula 1, Norris has shown rapid progress and has had standout performances on the track. He has achieved multiple podiums, including a second place in the 2020 Austrian Grand Prix. His aggressive driving style and ability to manage tires have earned him recognition in the category.

-Personality and Popularity: He has won the affection of fans for his outgoing personality, charisma, and active engagement on social media. He is known for his good sense of humor and his closeness to the sport's followers.

Accidents:

-2019 Austrian Grand Prix: He was involved in an incident on the first lap of the race, where he made contact with other cars at turn 4. The incident caused damage to his car and forced him to retire from the race.

-2020 Belgian Grand Prix: During qualifying, Norris had a crash at the Eau Rouge corner. The impact caused significant damage to his car, affecting his starting grid position for the race.

–**2021 Austrian Grand Prix:** On the final lap of the race, Norris was involved in an incident with Red Bull Racing driver, Sergio Pérez. There was contact between the two cars, causing Norris to lose several positions in the closing moments of the race.

Rivalries:

Lando Norris has not had notable rivalries or significant conflicts with other drivers in Formula 1.

As a young driver and relatively new to the category, Norris has focused on developing his career and establishing himself in the world of Formula 1.

Norris is known for his good relationship with his teammates and his friendly demeanor in the paddock.

He has shown respect and collaboration with other drivers on the track.

GEORGE RUSSELL

47

GEORGE RUSSELL.

He is a British racing driver born on February 15, 1998, in King's Lynn, England.

-Start in Motorsports: He began his career in karting and stood out as one of the most talented drivers of his generation. He won several national and international karting championships before moving to single-seater categories.

-European Formula 3 Championship: In 2017, Russell competed in the European Formula 3 Championship and won the title with the Prema Powerteam. His impressive track performances caught the eye and earned him recognition as a future talent in motorsport.

-Reserve and Lead Driver in Formula 1: Since 2017, Russell has been linked to the Mercedes young driver program. In 2019, he became Mercedes' reserve driver in Formula 1 and had the opportunity to compete in several free practice sessions.

-Williams Racing: In 2019, Russell was signed by the Williams Racing team as a lead driver in Formula 1. Although the team has struggled in terms of performance, Russell has showcased his skill and talent on multiple occasions and has been regarded as a driver with immense potential.

-Standout Performance at the 2020 Sakhir Grand Prix: At the 2020 Sakhir Grand Prix, Russell had the chance to replace Lewis Hamilton at Mercedes due to Hamilton's positive COVID-19 test. Russell impressed many with his performance, leading much of the race and showcasing his skill and speed. Despite not clinching the victory due to pit stop issues, his performance was highly praised.

-Other Achievements and Acknowledgments: In addition to his Formula 1 career, Russell has participated in other categories, like the Formula 2 Championship, where he also found success. He has been recognized as one of the most talented and promising young drivers in motorsport.

Accidents:

–2019 Belgian Grand Prix: On the first lap of the race, Russell was involved in an incident with the Alfa Romeo driver, Kimi Räikkönen. There was contact between the two cars, which resulted in damage to Russell's front wing and affected his performance in the race.

–2020 Tuscan Grand Prix: During a red flag and the subsequent race restart, Russell was involved in a chain-reaction crash in turn 2. Several cars collided, and Russell was among the drivers affected. His car sustained damage, and he had to retire from the race.

–2021 Hungarian Grand Prix: In qualifying, Russell had a crash at turn 14 after losing control of his car in rainy conditions. The accident caused damage to his car, forcing him to start from the pit lane in the race.

Rivalries:

George Russell has not had notable rivalries or significant conflicts with other drivers in Formula 1.

As a young and relatively new driver in the category, Russell has focused on developing his career and establishing himself in the world of Formula 1.

If you've enjoyed diving into the incredible stories
and thrilling feats of "Asphalt and Glory,"
we would love to ask you to share your
experience and write a review on Amazon.

Your feedback is invaluable to both us and other
Formula 1 enthusiasts looking to discover and
learn more about this exhilarating motorsport.

We understand that leaving a review requires a few
minutes of your time, but we encourage you to
share your thoughts and opinions with us.

Your support is essential for us to continue providing
quality content, as well as captivating stories and
intriguing facts about Formula 1 legends for
all lovers of the sport.

We genuinely appreciate your backing and hope you've
enjoyed reading about the fascinating races,
astonishing achievements, and intense
rivalries we've shared in this book.

Thank you for sharing your experience with us, and we
wish you many thrilling races and unforgettable
moments in Formula 1!

★ ★ ★ ★ ★

Printed in Great Britain
by Amazon

37072985R00096